First World War
and Army of Occupation
War Diary
France, Belgium and Germany

62 DIVISION
Headquarters, Branches and Services
Royal Army Veterinary Corps
Assistant Director Veterinary Services
and Assistant Provost Marshal
9 January 1917 - 31 August 1919

WO95/3074/3

The Naval & Military Press Ltd
www.nmarchive.com
Published in association with The National Archives

Published by

The Naval & Military Press Ltd

Unit 10 Ridgewood Industrial Park,

Uckfield, East Sussex,

TN22 5QE England

Tel: +44 (0) 1825 749494

www.naval-military-press.com

www.nmarchive.com

This diary has been reprinted in facsimile from the original. Any imperfections are inevitably reproduced and the quality may fall short of modern type and cartographic standards.

© **Crown Copyright**
Images reproduced by permission of The National Archives, London, England, 2015.

Contents

Document type	Place/Title	Date From	Date To
Heading	WO95/3074/3		
Heading	62nd Division Asst Dir. Vety Services Jan 1917-1919 Jun		
War Diary	Beaford	09/01/1917	09/01/1917
War Diary	Southampton	09/01/1917	09/01/1917
War Diary	Havre	10/01/1917	11/01/1917
War Diary	Auxi-Le-Chateau	12/01/1917	12/01/1917
War Diary	Frouen-Le-Grand	12/01/1917	21/01/1917
War Diary	Beaval	22/01/1917	22/01/1917
War Diary	Bus	23/01/1917	31/01/1917
Heading	War Diary A.D.M.S. 62nd Division Vol : 2 From 1-2-17 To 28-2-17		
War Diary	Bus	01/02/1917	07/02/1917
War Diary	Bus-Les-Artois	08/02/1917	03/03/1917
War Diary	Englebelmer	04/03/1917	01/04/1917
War Diary	Achiet Le Grand	02/04/1917	30/04/1917
Heading	War Diary of ADVS 62nd Division From 1-5-17 To 31-5-17 Volume 5		
War Diary	Achiet-Le-Grand	01/05/1917	31/05/1917
Heading	War Diary of A.D.V.S 62nd Division From 1st June 17 To 30th June 17 Volume VI		
War Diary	Achiet Le Grand	01/06/1917	15/06/1917
War Diary	Achille Le Patit	16/06/1917	28/06/1917
War Diary	Monument Commomoratif	29/06/1917	30/06/1917
Heading	War Diary of D.A.D.V.S 62nd Division From 1-7-17 To 31-7-17 Vol VII		
War Diary	Monument Commomoratif	01/07/1917	31/07/1917
Heading	War Diary of D.A.D.V.S From 1-8-17 To 31-8-17 Vol VIII		
War Diary	Monument Commomoratif	01/08/1917	31/08/1917
Heading	War Diary of D.A.D.V.S 62nd Division From 1-9-17 To 30-9-17 Volume IX		
War Diary	Monument Commomoratif	01/09/1917	30/09/1917
Heading	War Diary of D.A.D.V.S 62nd Division From 1-10-17 To 31-10-17 Volume X		
War Diary	Monument Commomoratif	01/10/1917	11/10/1917
War Diary	Haplincourt	12/10/1917	14/10/1917
War Diary	Camp of N.W. of Haplincourt	14/10/1917	29/10/1917
War Diary	Fosseux	30/10/1917	31/10/1917
Heading	War Diary of D.A.D.V.S 62nd Div From 1 XI 17 To 30 XI 17 Vol 11		
War Diary	Fosseux	01/11/1917	13/11/1917
War Diary	Haplincourt	14/11/1917	18/11/1917
War Diary	Barastre	19/11/1917	25/11/1917
War Diary	Neuville	26/11/1917	28/11/1917
War Diary	Haplincourt	29/11/1917	30/11/1917
Heading	War Diary of D.A.D.V.S 62nd Divn. From 1-12-17 To 31-12-17 Vol XII		
War Diary	Haplincourt	01/12/1917	03/12/1917
War Diary	Basseux	04/12/1917	05/12/1917

War Diary	Villers Chatel	06/12/1917	11/12/1917
War Diary	Labeuvriere	12/12/1917	18/12/1917
War Diary	Villers Chatel	19/12/1917	31/12/1917
Heading	War Diary of D.A.D.V.S 62nd (W.R) Dvn From 1-1-18 To 31-12-18 Vol XIII		
War Diary	Villers Chatel	01/01/1918	08/01/1918
War Diary	Victory Camp	09/01/1918	31/01/1918
Heading	War Diary of D.A.D.V.S 62nd (WR) Division From 1-2-18 To 28-2-18 Vol XIV		
War Diary	Victory Camp	01/02/1918	10/02/1918
War Diary	Villers Chatel	11/02/1918	28/02/1918
Heading	War Diary of D.A.D.V.S 62nd (W.R) Division From 1-3-18 To 31-3-18 Vol XV		
War Diary	Villers Chatel	01/03/1918	03/03/1918
War Diary	Roclincourt	04/03/1918	24/03/1918
War Diary	Warlus	25/03/1918	31/03/1918
Heading	War Diary of D.A.D.V.S 62nd (W.R) Division Vol XVI From 1 4/18 To 30 4/18		
War Diary	Warlus	01/04/1918	01/04/1918
War Diary	Pas	02/04/1918	06/04/1918
War Diary	Henu	07/04/1918	16/04/1918
War Diary	Pas	17/04/1918	23/04/1918
War Diary	Authie	24/04/1918	30/04/1918
Heading	War Diary of D.A.D.V.S 62nd (W.R) Dvn From 1-5-18 To 30-5-18 Vol XVII		
War Diary	Authie	01/05/1918	16/05/1918
War Diary	Pas	17/05/1918	26/05/1918
War Diary	Pas En Artois	27/05/1918	31/05/1918
Heading	War Diary of D.A.D.V.S 62nd (W.R) Div From 1 6/18 To 30 6/18 Vol XVIII		
War Diary	Las-en-Artois	01/06/1918	30/06/1918
Heading	War Diary of D.A.D.V.S 62nd (W.R) Division Vol : XVIV From 1-7-17 To 31-7-17		
War Diary	Pas En Artois	01/07/1918	15/07/1918
War Diary	Mailly Le Camp	16/07/1918	16/07/1918
War Diary	Vraux	17/07/1918	17/07/1918
War Diary	Tours Sur Marne	18/07/1918	31/07/1918
Heading	War Diary of D.A.D.V.S 62nd (W.R) Dvn From 1-8-18 To 31-8-18 Vol : XX		
War Diary	Tours Sur Marne	01/08/1918	01/08/1918
War Diary Miscellaneous	Bisseuil	03/08/1918	04/08/1918
War Diary	Pas-En-Artois	05/08/1918	14/08/1918
War Diary	Authis	15/08/1918	18/08/1918
War Diary	Grenas	19/08/1918	19/08/1918
War Diary	Bavincourt	20/08/1918	21/08/1918
War Diary	Doullens	22/08/1918	23/08/1918
War Diary	Bienvillers	24/08/1918	30/08/1918
War Diary	Douchy	31/08/1918	31/08/1918
Heading	War Diary of D.A.D.V.S 62nd (W.R) Dvn From 1-9-18 To 30-9-18 Vol XXI		
War Diary	Douchy-Les-Ayette	01/09/1918	03/09/1918
War Diary	Courcelles	04/09/1918	11/09/1918
War Diary	Fremicourt	11/09/1918	14/09/1918
War Diary	Gomiecourt	15/09/1918	30/09/1918

Heading	War Diary of D.A.D.V.S 62nd (WR) Dvn From 1-10-18 To 31-10-18 Vol XXII		
War Diary	Gomiecourt	01/10/1918	03/10/1918
War Diary	Hermies	04/10/1918	08/10/1918
War Diary	Flesquires	09/10/1918	09/10/1918
War Diary	Masnieres	10/10/1918	10/10/1918
War Diary	Estourmel	11/10/1918	17/10/1918
War Diary	Bevillers	18/10/1918	30/10/1918
War Diary	Solesmes	31/10/1918	31/10/1918
Heading	War Diary of D.A.D.V.S 62nd (W.R) Dvn From 1-11-18 To 30-11-18 Vol XXIII		
War Diary	Solesmes	01/11/1918	03/11/1918
War Diary	Escarmain	04/11/1918	04/11/1918
War Diary	Frasnoy	05/11/1918	07/11/1918
War Diary	Le Trechon	08/11/1918	09/11/1918
War Diary	Hautmont	10/11/1918	10/11/1918
War Diary	Sous Le Bois	11/11/1918	17/11/1918
War Diary	Ham Sur Haure	18/11/1918	20/11/1918
War Diary	Loverval	21/11/1918	24/11/1918
War Diary	Bioul	25/11/1918	26/11/1918
War Diary	Leignon	27/11/1918	30/11/1918
Heading	War Diary of D.A.D.V.S 62nd (W.R) Dvn Vol.: XXIV From 1-12-18 To 31-12-18		
War Diary	Leignon	01/12/1918	13/12/1918
War Diary	Vielsalm	14/12/1918	16/12/1918
War Diary	Malmedy	17/12/1918	21/12/1918
War Diary	Schleiden	22/12/1918	31/12/1918
Heading	War Diary of D.A.D.V.S 62nd (W.R) Dvn From 1-1-19 To 31-1-19 Volume XXV		
War Diary	Schleiden	01/01/1919	31/01/1919
Heading	War Diary of D.A.D.V.S 62nd (WR) Dvn From 1-2-19 To 28-2-19 Vol XXVI		
War Diary	Schleiden	01/02/1919	28/02/1919
Heading	War Diary of D.A.D.V.S Highland Dvn From 1-3-19 To 31-3-19 Vol XXVII		
War Diary	Sehleiden	01/03/1919	12/03/1919
War Diary	Duren	13/03/1919	31/03/1919
War Diary	Schleiden	01/03/1919	12/03/1919
War Diary	Duren	13/03/1919	31/03/1919
Miscellaneous	To Officer i/c. R at V.C Records Woolwich	08/05/1919	08/05/1919
Heading	War Diary of D.A.D.V.S Highland Division From 1.4.19 To 30.4.19 Vol XXVIII		
War Diary	Duren	01/04/1919	30/04/1919
Heading	War Diary of D.A.D.V.S Highland Division From 1.5.19 To 31.5.19 Vol XXIX		
War Diary	Kreuzau	01/05/1919	14/05/1919
War Diary	Kreuzau	16/05/1919	31/05/1919
Heading	War Diary of D.A.D.V.S Highland Division From 1-5-19 To 31-5-19 Vol XXIX		
War Diary	Kreuzau	01/05/1919	14/05/1919
War Diary	Kreuzau	16/05/1919	31/05/1919
Heading	War Diary of D.A.D.V.S Highland Division From 1.6.19 To 30.6.19 Vol XXVIII		
War Diary	Kreuzau	01/06/1919	30/06/1919
Heading	War Diary of D.A.D.V.S Highland Division From 1.6.19 To 30.6.19 Vol XXVIII		

War Diary	Kreuzau	01/06/1919	30/06/1919
Heading	War Diary of D.A.D.V.S Highland Division From 1st July 1919 To 31st July 1919 (Volume XXVII)		
War Diary	Kreuzau	01/07/1919	31/07/1919
Heading	War Diary of D.A.D.V.S Highland Division From 1.8.19 To 31.8.19 Volume XXXII		
War Diary	Kreuzau	01/08/1919	11/08/1919
War Diary	Clipstone	12/08/1919	31/08/1919

WO95/30744/3

62ND DIVISION

ASST. DIR. VETY SERVICES.

JAN 1917 - ~~DEC 1918~~ 1919 JUN

Original

Army Form C. 2118.

WAR DIARY
or
INTELLIGENCE SUMMARY.

(Erase heading not required.)

Instructions regarding War Diaries and Intelligence Summaries are contained in F. S. Regs, Part II. and the Staff Manual respectively. Title pages will be prepared in manuscript.

of A.D.V.S. 62nd Division.

Place	Date	Hour	Summary of Events and Information	Remarks and references to Appendices
Bedford	Tuesday 9/1/17	9.15am	62nd Divisional A.D.V.S. left for Southampton by train	cpt
Southampton	"	5.30pm	Arrived	cpt
do	"	9.30pm	Departure by Transport Arromanches	cpt
Havre	10/1/17	2 pm	Arrived	cpt
do	11/1/17	3.30pm	Departure by train	cpt
Amiens & Chatam	12/1/17	3.30pm	Arrived	cpt
Fienvillers at Frevent	12/1/17	6.30pm	Do	cpt
do	13/1/17	3 pm	Reported personally to Col. A.E. D.D.V.S. 3rd Army S. 7.101.	cpt
do	14/1/17 to		Received reports from 2nd Army & Cav. Corps. Dist. H.Q.s. - Inspection of M.V.S. Mobile in arrangements, inspection 576 Co., Lynx Co., ascending from 61 Div. M.V.	cpt
do	15/1/17	—	Distribution of V.O.s arranged, inspection 576 Co., Lynx Co., ascending from 61 Div. M.V. with 62nd M.V.S., Dy. 16 20 as Depot of animal carcasses, wrote D.D.V.S. Army re. remounts.	cpt
do	16/1/17	—	Dis. at A.D.M.S. 60 awaiting interview Brig. Major RA re V.Os interview V.Os attend at Forces in Field	cpt
do	17/1/17		Visit to Lieut. Carter Doullens re M.V.S.	
do	18/1/17		Conference of V.Os returning Remington, visit of Major Camden A.D.V.S. 5th Army	
do	19/1/17		Visit to 311 Brig. Outletters 315 Brig. R.F.A. occasion arrangements for eviscerating of east horses for evacuation to Abbeville	

T.131. Wt. W708—776. 500000. 4/15. Sir J. C. & S.

Original

Army Form C. 2118.

WAR DIARY
or
INTELLIGENCE SUMMARY.
(Erase heading not required.)

of ADVS 62 Division

Instructions regarding War Diaries and Intelligence Summaries are contained in F. S. Regs., Part II. and the Staff Manual respectively. Title pages will be prepared in manuscript.

No. 62nd (W.R.) DIVN. A.D.V.S.

Place	Date	Hour	Summary of Events and Information	Remarks and references to Appendices
From le Grand	20.1.17	30-40	Arrangements for transport of sick horses to R.T.O. Bouquemaison 3.0 pm 21.1.17	
Do	21.1.17		Inspection of my 30 horses in M.V.S. 1 died during night. 2. 6. to be destroyed by my 6 M.V.S. Inspection of mares	
Beaval	22.1.17		Moved to Beauval	
Bus	23.1.17		Bus to Bus the action	
"	24.1.17		Telegraphed location to DDVS	
"	25.1.17		A.D.M.S. re 10% toting of horses, wired DDVS re ditto 4/10. A.D.P.S. & army called at 10.30 & arranged that M.V.S. attend remain at Bus as Area was occupied by M.V.S. 32nd Division. Major Cowden interviewed Q re this re ditto. Visited horse lines of A.S.C. at commencement line, water very scarce & horse lane. G.S. for mules to work on a/c of purpose see long program. Recommended 2 lbs of bran pr 25lb H.D. and 1 lb/pr gun horses/unfed old horse H.Q.Q. r Signal Co. T.O. conference at 2.30 Captn. Muth absent sent him to leave. Mr Dixon was instructed to proceed for duty as D.M.C. at Orion tomorrow	
"	26.1.17		Returns prepared	
"	27.1.17		Mobile Vet Section moved into greater line of 32nd Division Went to Reserve via A.D.C. Flore, first 2 motor ambulance arranged Hathorn res	

Original

Vol I

Army Form C. 2118.

WAR DIARY
or
INTELLIGENCE SUMMARY.   ADMS 62nd Division

(Erase heading not required.)

Instructions regarding War Diaries and Intelligence Summaries are contained in F. S. Regs., Part II. and the Staff Manual respectively. Title pages will be prepared in manuscript.

Place	Date	Hour	Summary of Events and Information	Remarks and references to Appendices
Rue	29/1/17		Visited Hors lines of 311 Brigade & 312th Brigade at Lonnement inspected horses in M.V.S. for evacuation to Base.	
"	30/1/17		Some of horses left behind on march sent to D.T.VS. Major Taylor A.D.V.S. 62nd Division went to hospital & handed over the duties to Capt Abrams A.V.C. 62nd Divisional M.V.S. duty Section.	
"	31/1/17		List of horses evacuated to No 22 Base Veterinary Hospital sent to D.D.V.S. 5th Army.	(Sd) Abrams Capt AVC for ADVS 62nd Division

(Sd) Abrams Capt AVC
for ADVS 62nd Division

Original

War Diary
A.A.S. 62nd Division
Vol. 2 From 1~2~19 to 28~2~19.

Vol 2

Army Form C. 2118.

WAR DIARY
or
INTELLIGENCE SUMMARY.
(Erase heading not required.)

Original

Instructions regarding War Diaries and Intelligence Summaries are contained in F.S. Regs., Part II. and the Staff Manual respectively. Title pages will be prepared in manuscript.

F.A.D.V.S. 62nd Division

Place	Date	Hour	Summary of Events and Information	Remarks and references to Appendices
Bus.	1/7		Capt Aken acting ADVS went to Bernerd, inspected ADVS charges, found same in state of collapse with ADVS Prunceras (see 2/7) Interviews with staffs 3rd Army.	
"	2/7		Visit to 312th Bac R.F.A. Convenient, inspected Mange camps, also ADVS Interviews with staff 3rd Army.	
"	3/7		Visit to Headquarters of Division at Bus & units in Bus.	
"	4/7		ADVS inspected H.Q. in reference to Mange Cases Collected. Also 312th Bac R.F.A. at Convenient. ADVS took arrangements with No. Ho Army re D.O. for 311th Bac R.F.A. Capt Paul to move with Red Brigade. Instructions received not to evacuate any animals until further notice, units to retain their animals.	
"	6/7		Capt Aken for ADVS inspects all animals in the 311th Bac R.F.A. at Achiet.	
"	7/8		Visit No. 46 V.T.S. French glass dumps & evacuees to h.w.s. for evacuation.	

P. Aken Capt. AVC
For ADVS 62nd Division

Original

WAR DIARY
or
INTELLIGENCE SUMMARY.
(Erase heading not required.)

Army Form C. 2118.

A.D.V.S. 63rd Division

Place	Date	Hour	Summary of Events and Information	Remarks and references to Appendices
Bruaylepin	8.2.17		Reported for duty with the 63rd Division as A.D.V.S. on instructions from the D.D.V.S. 5th Army	
	9.2.17		Attended at Rainneval a conference of A.D.V.S's and there discussed the prevention and spread of Mange. Visited the 3/1 West Riding Mobile Veterinary Section	
			Had a Conference with V.O. of the Division at my Office in Bros. Visited and inspected the horses of the 3/1 M.V.S., the 6th Labour Battalion, and the horses of the Head Quarters of the Division	
	10.2.17		Inspected the horses of the 311th Bde R.F.A. at Horses Louis Molienes. These animals are in fair condition, with the exception of a few debility cases. There was one case of suspected Mange which was being sent to M.V.S. The horses that have been clipped recently have condition regularly owing to the severe weather after having been accustomed to good stabling in England. Visited and inspected the horses of the D.A.C. Nearly all the animals in the four sections are looking well. There were two cases of suspected Mange on N°1 Section & N°3 Section 1 case and N°4 section 13 cases. V.O./c received instructions to send these horses to M.V.S. Capt. Brown reported for duty from 31st Division vice Capt. Brown who has been instructed to report O.C. 29nd Base Vet'y Hospital.	
	11.2.17		Proceeded to Tournanvent & inspected the horses of 31st Bde. The horses of this Bde are in fair condition C.Bty seems thinner than any of the others. V.O./c instructed to send 3 cases suspected mange to M.V.S. from B Battery	

T.131. W1. W708-776. 500000. 4/15. Sir J. C. & 9.

WAR DIARY or INTELLIGENCE SUMMARY

Army Form C. 2118.

Original
A.D.V.S.
62nd Division

Place	Date	Hour	Summary of Events and Information	Remarks and references to Appendices
Bus les Artois	11.2.17		Captain Moran A.V.C. left for 23rd Base Vety Hospital. Inspected horses of the following units at Couremont. 2/6 West Yorks. 2/6 Duke of Wellingtons. The animals in both units are looking well. Visited the M.F.B.	
	12.2.17		Visited the D.A.C. and inspected horses of new Battery. Had arrived on the night of the 10th & join the 311th Bde R.F.A. Three cases of anaemic "incardial" mange cases in Jos Section. Shoeities to Arborane and inspected horses of new Battery. Had arrived on the night of the 10th & join the 311th Bde R.F.A. Three cases of anaemic range was isolated & instructions given as to precautions to take to prevent spread of disease. Upwards of 70 horses of this Battery are suffering from "sore back". D.D.V.S. called and discussed treatment of mange etc. Inspected horses Mr Shed Quartes.	
	13.2.17		Visited and inspected the horses of the 1st Company's Divisional Train. Six Signal Company. Proceeded to Pas and inspected the horses of "A" & "C" Batteries of Ledger and 2/6 Ypres Kings at Engrave. Inspected the animals of the above units and looking well more particularly the Team horses drawing the heavy wort they are doing.	
	14.2.17		Had a meeting of NCO's of the division to give a Demonstration of the new "Eye test" of Mallusin for Glanders. Proceeded to Souastre and inspected the horses of the 3rd Field Company of Engineers.	
	15.2.17		Inspected the horses of the 2/1 Field Ambulances at Bus, also the horses of the 310 Bde R.F.A. Vandeillers. The animals in this Brigade are in good condition, also that of the 2/1 Field Ambulance.	

Army Form C. 2118.

WAR DIARY
or
INTELLIGENCE SUMMARY.   A.D.V.S. 62nd Division
(Erase heading not required.)

Instructions regarding War Diaries and Intelligence Summaries are contained in F.S. Regs., Part II. and the Staff Manual respectively. Title pages will be prepared in manuscript.

Original

Place	Date	Hour	Summary of Events and Information	Remarks and references to Appendices
Beaul. Arbin	16.2.17		Had a meeting of Veterinary Officers and discussed the precautions as to the further spread of mange. Attended at Divisional Hd.Qrs. on indicator and had an interview with D.D.V.S. providing	
	17.2.17		Proceeded to horse lines of the D.A.C. and inspected to Western animals indicating sore suspicion there. Visited Beaucourt and inspected horses of the following units 2/5, 2/6, 2/7, 2/8 West Yorks Regiments. 3 cases of suspected mange in 2/8 West Yorks were pieced out & isolated. Instructions were given as to how to prevent further spread of the disease. Inspected horses of the 2/1 Field Ambulance at Bertincourt.	
	18.2.17		Proceeded & shortly made respective horses in the following units that were Mallein tested on the 17th Inst. 457, 460, 461 Companys R.E. a total of 141 animals had been tested no reactors. Visited Salient suspects 30 animals that were Mallein tested 17 Inst. Captain Hill A.V.C. reported at this office under instructions from A.D.V.S. 9th Division. This officer is i/c of Same units of the 9th Division stationed in this area. Visited the 62nd Divisional M.V. Inspection animals for evacuation on the 19th	
	19.2.17		The A.D.V.S. 5th Army called at this office & made inquiries as to spread of mange. Proceeded to Vaucelles. Inspected horses of 310th Bde R.F.A. Mallein'd the previous day there were no reactors. Inspected horses of B Battery 310th Bde R.F.A. many animals in this battery very debilitated. V.O.(AR) Mobile Vety Section instructed to move on the 20th to Gorenflos.	

WAR DIARY of INTELLIGENCE SUMMARY

Army Form C. 2118.

F.O.V.S. 62nd Division

Place	Date	Hour	Summary of Events and Information	Remarks and references to Appendices
Bus Lés Artois	20.2.17		Proceeded to Mailly Maillet and inspected horses of the 457, 460 & 461 Companys R.E. stationed on the 19th inst. Visited Vauchellers & inspected 2 horses of Battery 307 Bde stationed on 19th. Visits at Waggon Lines 10 A.C. inspected 253 horses stationed yesterday. 2/(H.R.) Mobile Vet Section moved to Forceville. Notice that horses at all low any condition mainly because stabletedted T in enemy area are mounting owing to hard weather & exposure. Capt Wrectou had 4 days forced leave.	
	21.2.17		Visited the Waggon Lines of the 312th Bde R.F.A. Companies and inspected 262 horses stallion teated the previous day. there were no reactors. Proceeded to Forceville and visited the 2/(H.R.) Mobile Vet Section. Several horses in the 312th & 13th Bde R.F.A. being in a debilitation condition instructions were given to send them to M.V.S. for evacuation	
	22.2.17		Visited the Lines Lines of the D.A.C. and examined all the animals of No.1 Section stallioned the previous day. Proceeded to the horse lines of 311 Bde R.F.A. at Louvencourt & examined all horses stallioned on 21/2/17. Owing to there and rain the horses standing in the open are suffering a great deal from the mud & exposure	
	23.2.17		Day visited the 2/(H.R.) M.V. Section at Forceville and inspected horses for evacuation. Proceeded to Labillers & inspected horses of 63rd Divisional Train, a good few of these animals are in very condition owing in a great measure to hard work and that in consequence caused by long journey to Railhead	
	24.2.17		Visited at Mailly Maillet the horse lines of the 457, 460 & 461 Companys R.E. no further cases of mange in 461 Company	

Army Form C. 2118.

WAR DIARY
of
INTELLIGENCE SUMMARY.

A.D.V.S.
63rd Division

(Erase heading not required.)

Original

Instructions regarding War Diaries and Intelligence Summaries are contained in F. S. Regs., Part II. and the Staff Manual respectively. Title pages will be prepared in manuscript.

Place	Date	Hour	Summary of Events and Information	Remarks and references to Appendices
Beaumont-Hamel	24.2.17		Inspected the horses of the 186th Infantry Bde at Bolton Camp & Ouldern Camp. Inspected horses of Artillery horses Picts at Ourinval & G.rs	
	25.2.17		The 10.10.V.S accompanied by the D.D.V.S and myself inspected the horses of the 310th Bde R.F.A at Vardellos. The 312th Bde R.F.A at Louvencourt, also the 311th Bde R.F.A. The D.A.C horses since my visit but no inspection took place owing to the majority of the animals being out on duty.	
	26.2.17		Inspected horses stabled belonging to Divisional 4 Coys H.Q. Head Quarters R.E and Divisional Signal Coys. Visited Beauvoirt Railhead & saw animals evacuated by 74 (W.R) Mobile Veterinary Section.	
	27.2.17		Proceeded to Forceville inspected horses (at T.M.Bde) M.V.S for evacuation or 58th. Visited Ottolsens and Bolton Camps and inspected horses of the 186th Infy Brigade. Inspected at Forceville H.3 (W.R) Field Ambulance host. The animals shows signs of great fatigue owing to the heavy work.	
	28.2.17		Visited the horse lines of the 311th & 313th R.F.A Brigades at Louvencourt. The majority of the horses have moved to a new location. Those left behind are debility or sick animals. The former are improving after spared clothing & rest. Where practicable nose-bags are being over worked & up to now on a reduced ration. Evacuation animals in most wards are likely to be great unless something is done to relieve the work of the animals on the Division are suffering from great disadvantage not having been accustomed to the exposure hitherto having a more plentiful ration & less work	

E.T. Niell Capt. A.V.C
A.D.V.S.
63rd Division

VOLUME III
A.D.V.S.
63rd Division

Vol 3

Original

WAR DIARY
of
INTELLIGENCE SUMMARY.
(Erase heading not required.)

Army Form C. 2118.

Instructions regarding War Diaries and Intelligence Summaries are contained in F. S. Regs., Part II. and the Staff Manual respectively. Title pages will be prepared in manuscript.

Place	Date	Hour	Summary of Events and Information	Remarks and references to Appendices
Beaulencourt	1.3.17		Visited the horse lines at Bolton Camp of the 188th, 186 and 189 Infantry Brigades. Although doing a lot of hard work the animals of these Brigade are looking very fit. Visited the horse lines of the M.A.C. but found them on the move to a new location. Have written instructions to D.D.V.S. on inspection of horse standings and stables in Englebelmer area as the (63rd) Division recently occupying this location suffered greatly from mange.	
	2.3.17		Visited the horse lines of the No. 1 Field Ambulance at Acheux. These animals on the mend on clipping, some are slightly affected with mange. energetic steps are being taken to arrest further increase. Proceeded to Mailly Maillet and inspected horses of the 461st Company R.E. a further increase of mange has occurred almost next ... road next. There are only slightly affected and with a few dressings a tropic recovery should be effected. Visited the 141st HAR Field Ambulance saw one case of mange which is now almost cured. Visited at Beaucourt the horses of the 311th Bde. R.F.A. The majority of the animals in this brigade are in condition rapidly owing to the present steamy weather.	
	3.3.17		Proceeded to Trainvilles and inspected animals for evacuation on 7/6th M.V.S. also animals of the 308 Machine Gun Company that have joined this Division.	
Englebelmer	4.3.17	10.30 am	Moved from Bus-les-Artes and arrived at Englebelmer at 1.30 pm. Inspected billets horses of 314th Bde. these animals could have quickly improved had they been under Shelter, but being in the open I am afraid there is little hope	

Army Form C. 2118.

WAR DIARY
of
INTELLIGENCE SUMMARY.

(Erase heading not required.)

A.D.V.S.
6th Division.

Instructions regarding War Diaries and Intelligence Summaries are contained in F.S. Regs., Part II. and the Staff Manual respectively. Title pages will be prepared in manuscript.

Place	Date	Hour	Summary of Events and Information	Remarks and references to Appendices
Englebelmer	5.3.17		Inspected 3 Battery's of the 31st Bde R.F.A. at waggon lines south of Englebelmer. Proceeded to Auchonvillers to waggon lines C Battery 311th Bde R.F.A. the animals in this Battery are in a very bad condition of the bad work and severe weather conditions. I am afraid many animals will die. The horses of this Brigade as a whole are going down in condition quickly. Inspected at the waggon lines the horses of the 30th Bde R.F.A. All the animals in this Bde are standing the severe weather of the 311th on 311 Bde	
"	6.3.17		Proceeded to Forceville and inspected 2/3 Field Ambulance horses also animals of 208th M.S. Company in same village. Inspected animals for evacuation in 7/(6R) M.V. at Forceville. Inspected the horses & mules of the 184 Infantry Bde. Capt Cross reported at this Office on his return from leave. Animals in all units without Shelter are suffering greatly from the severe weather	
"	7.3.17		Had a visit from the D.D.V.S. in reference to a letter pointing out that horses were dying in great numbers owing to exhaustion from over work and exposure. The D.D.V.S. self received C Battery 311th Bde R.F.A. this unit is almost immobile through animals succumbing to hard work and exposure. I proceeded to lines lines 311th Bde R.F.A. hardly inoculated Capt Marshs to evacuate "Debility" cases of the animals sure young.	
"	8.3.17		Visits the 2/(6R) M.V. at Forceville. Inspected 2 cases of Suspected Mange in M.S. Machine Gun Corps. This kind belongs to 11th Division	

T.134. Wt. W708—776. 600000. 4/15. Sir J. C. & S.

Army Form C. 2118.

WAR DIARY
of
INTELLIGENCE SUMMARY.
(Erase heading not required.)

A.D.V.S.
63rd Division

Instructions regarding War Diaries and Intelligence Summaries are contained in F.S. Regs., Part II. and the Staff Manual respectively. Title pages will be prepared in manuscript.

Place	Date	Hour	Summary of Events and Information	Remarks and references to Appendices
Englebelmer	8.3.17		Vaudet the horse lines of the D.A.C. at Hamel, also inspected horses of the 311th Bde R.F.A. at the same place. As a result of the severe weather last night a great many animals suffering from debility and exhaustion die. The percentage of death is grave. No man is taken some steps are taken to relieve the horse animals of work and provide shelter. I am of the opinion 80 p.c. of these suffer. The above remarks refer principally to Artillery & A.S.C. Examiner Corps remounts sent to Head Quarters demands of a very insufficient class received. Stamps must work. Two remount mules sent to A.V.S. from A.S.C. suspected of mange.	
"	9.3.17		To day visited the horse lines of Divisional Train & Englebelmer inspected remounts received on the day previous, most of the other horses were out at work. Vaudet at Hamel the 311th Bde R.F.A. also the D.A.C. and inspected remounts received by these units. If the present severe weather continues there is no doubt there remounts will fall away greatly in condition more particularly on account of their clipped appearance.	
"	10.3.17		The S.Q.M.S. made a raid today and inspected the horses on the following units in the Division 310, 311, 317, Brigades of Artillery the D.A.C. and part of the A.S.C. Train. Several horses in low condition were picked out for examination. The weather so much milder today but an appreciable brighter appearance is noticeable in all the animals.	
"	11.3.17		Vaudet at Forceville the M.M.P. M.V.S. and inspected animals for evacuation on the 12th	

T.131. W⁴. W708-776. 500000. 4/15. Sir J. C. & S.

Army Form C. 2118.

WAR DIARY
of
INTELLIGENCE SUMMARY.
A.D.V.S.
62nd Division

(Erase heading not required.)

Instructions regarding War Diaries and Intelligence Summaries are contained in F. S. Regs., Part II. and the Staff Manual respectively. Title pages will be prepared in manuscript.

Place	Date	Hour	Summary of Events and Information	Remarks and references to Appendices
Engelbelmer	11.3.17		Inspected at Engelbelmer the "A Company" of divisional train horses at Hoppe Lines also inspected at Engelbelmer the horses of the 184th Infantry Brigade	
"	12.3.17		Visited Hamel and inspected the animals of the D.A.C and 311th Brigade R.F.A. There are some debilitated animals in these units, but slowly the weather improves and no additional hours given them. I am sure these would be a decided improvement shortly. There still remain a few cases of mange in D.A.C. but it does not appear to be spreading	
	13.3.17		Visited at Forceville 311 (NB) R.F.A and inspected animals for evacuation on the M.T. Inspected animals of the 312 & 313rd Medium Trun (Company) that arrived recently. Inspected horses of C Battery 311 Bde R.F.A at Mailly Maillet. There are still some very thin animals in this Battery.	
	14.3.17		Visited and inspected at Hamel the animals of the D.A.C. mentioned on the 13th inst. Inspected horses of 311 Bde R.F.A. at Hamel. There are still a few debilitated animals in the latter Bde and of the hard work required Continues Inspection Insurepoles a further high feeling.	
	15.3.17		Visited inspected horses at Mailly Wood belonging to No. 1 (Company) R.E the mange cases in this unit "practically cured". Visited inspected horses of 2/3 Field Ambulance at Acheux. Many cases in this unit showing splendidly	
	16.3.17		Visited the horse lines of the 312th Brigade R.F.A at Mailly Wood. Inspected all the animals. There are still a few very thin debilitated animals	

WAR DIARY of INTELLIGENCE SUMMARY.

Army Form C. 2118.

(Erase heading not required.)

A.D.F.S. 8th Division

Place	Date	Hour	Summary of Events and Information	Remarks and references to Appendices
Englebelmer	17.3.17		Visited hourly inspected horses of the 311th Bde R.F.A. inspected of harness inspected horses cases of the 40th & 41st Companys R.E. at hourly tested. Visited at Hamel inspected horses in 311th Bde R.F.A. and D.A.C.	
"	18.3.17		Visited at Forceville 2/1 (W.R.) M.T. inspected animals for evacuation on the 19th inst. Inspected all the Wagon Lines Englebelmer the horses of the 2nd Bde R.F.A.	
"	19.3.17		Visited inspected the horses of the 311th Bde at Hamel a few debility cases are being evacuated no decided improvement in the animals else to improvement in the weather. Visited inspected the 406th and 461st Companys R.E. horses at Beaumont also 51st Machine Gun Company.	
"	20.3.17		Visited and inspected at Beaumont the horses of the 2nd 3rd Bde R.F.A. & few inspected mange cases that are under treatment have improved. there cases are doing well. There are still a good few then animals in this Brigade who hope they will improve with better weather. Inspected horses of the 16th Infantry Bde at different points between Beaumont & Beaucourt. Inspected the horses of 3 Companys of the Pioneer these animals show a decided improvement. Though still doing very hard work. Proceeded to Hamel to select a site for the M.V.S. which is moving there on the 22nd inst. There is not much choice on side S, but I have chosen the one that protects from the winds &c has a good Water system	
"	21.3.17		Visited the 2/1 (W.R.) M.V.S. at Forceville and Examined horses for evacuation.	

Army Form C. 2118.

WAR DIARY
of
INTELLIGENCE SUMMARY.
(Erase heading not required.)

F.D.V.S. 1/2 nd Division

Instructions regarding War Diaries and Intelligence Summaries are contained in F.S. Regs., Part II. and the Staff Manual respectively. Title pages will be prepared in manuscript.

Place	Date	Hour	Summary of Events and Information	Remarks and references to Appendices
Englebelmer	22.3.17		Proceeded to Forceville to 1/1/5 R.J. M.V.S. in reference to their moving to Hamel. Inspected horse of A/8 Field Ambulance at Forceville. Inspected horse of the 528 Company of Divisional Train. Inspected horse of the 4th Yorks I amce Station R.D. Beaumont. Visited the new site at Hamel for M.V.S. Mobile Vet'y Section moved to Hamel.	
"	23.3.17		Inspected horses Divisional Headquarters. Proceeded to Hamel inspected horses a section of the 129th Company A.S.C. Auxiliary Horse Transport attached to this Division. Inspected at the M.V.S. Hamel 25 debility cases sent in by 311th Bde R.J.A. prior to leaving this division to join 3rd Army. Visited R.J.O. at Beaucourt made arrangements for evacuation from M.V.S. Captain Sanders left the Division having gone with the 311th Bde. R.J.A. Inspected the 460th Company R.E.'s at Beaucourt also the 74th West Yorks animals in both units looking fairly well. Procured 6 transport inspected suitable site for M.V.S.	
"	24.3.17		Proceeded to Englebelmer and inspected horses of the 311th Bde. R.J.A. all their animals have been over worked so much so that I now consider the Brigade in a state of immobility. The horses in C Battery are the worst. Between 50 + 60 animals of this brigade will have to be evacuated. Visited + inspected horses of B/311th Bde R.J.A. about 40 in each Battery will have to be evacuated for absolute. Generally the horses in this brigade have started the trying times well. The horses in the 461st Company R.E.'s have also been over worked the Kit+ remount of them are losing condition	

WAR DIARY
or
INTELLIGENCE SUMMARY.
(Erase heading not required.)

Army Form C. 2118.

A.D.V.S.
62nd Division

Place	Date	Hour	Summary of Events and Information	Remarks and references to Appendices
Engelbelmer	26.3.17		Proceeded to Leabritiers and inspected 16 animals left by G.Coy, began by the 311 H Bde R.H.A. Army Train. Messengers were enquiring from Veterinary Officers re disability and Exhaustion. On debility of the 61 two asst. one animal suffering from Catarrhal dishayer as there was no hope of Recovery. Inspected the 2/2 and 2/3 Feld Ambulance horses at Acheux & Forceville respectively.	
"	27.3.17		Proceeded to Leabritiers made arrangements for examining 14 animals of the 311 H Bde mentioned above. Visited the horse lines of the D.A.C. East meanwhile, inspected the animals of the 3 Sections. Although somewhat Thinner than animals have about the Trying Line better than the Artillery	
"	28.3.17		Visited & inspected the horses of the 460 and 457 (Company) R.E at Acheux le Petit and the 447 Company R.E at Acheux le Grand. The Animals in the latter Company show more signs of hard work than the other two Companys. Inspected at Hornement the 555 Company ASC train also at Same place the Food York animals. The horses in both Trains made one having Exhibition	
"	29.3.17		Visited the 71 678 A.T.S at Haval	
"			Visited 71 678 A.T.S at Haval and inspected 2 animals for evacuation. Was visited by the O.T.I.S S.Army whereupon the question of animals in the Division in regard to debility, mange, etc	
"	30.3.17		Proceeded to Haval and inspected animals at A.T.S for evacuation on the 31.3.17	

Army Form C. 2118.

WAR DIARY
or
INTELLIGENCE SUMMARY.
(Erase heading not required.)

A.D.V.S.
61st Division

Instructions regarding War Diaries and Intelligence Summaries are contained in F. S. Regs., Part II. and the Staff Manual respectively. Title pages will be prepared in manuscript.

Place	Date	Hour	Summary of Events and Information	Remarks and references to Appendices
Englebelmer	30.3.17		Had a meeting of Veterinary Officers at my office & discussed the measures of precaution to be taken for stabling horses in houses or shelters used by the enemy also to inspect all sanitary arrangements. A copy of the wire in reference to "Glanders" & spread of same by agents of the enemy in French horses has been given to each V.O.	
"	31.3.17		Visited at Acheux the Stables of the 2/3 Field Ambulance has evacuated from this unit. Visited and inspected the horses of the 2/3 Field Ambulance at Forceville. His cases of Geopyrotes Mange making good progress under recovery. Inspected animals of the Divisional Signal Company R.E. at Englebelmer. During the month the wastage has been high, or known of this Division. The Causes (1 Horses broken 3 cononed 3 bad Roads) have been enumerated, reported on to D.D.Q. and D.D.V.S. Army. Debility is rather on the increase owing to the shortage of animals, two causing double work on the remainder.	

J.R. Nell Major A.V.O
A.D.V.S. 61st Division

Original

VOL. IV

Army Form C. 2118.

WAR DIARY
of
~~INTELLIGENCE SUMMARY.~~

F.A.D.S.
63rd Division

Vol 4

Instructions regarding War Diaries and Intelligence Summaries are contained in F. S. Regs., Part II. and the Staff Manual respectively. Title pages will be prepared in manuscript.

(Erase heading not required.)

Place	Date	Hour	Summary of Events and Information	Remarks and references to Appendices
Englebelmer	1.4.19		Visited 3/(1st)R.I. at Hamel. Proceeded to Achiet le Grand and selected a second site for A.D.S. the previous place chosen being taken by A.D.M.S. Visited and inspected the horses of the 310 T Bde at Ligignies. The animals of this Bde are standing this severe weather rather well except D Battery animals, a good number are very low in condition.	
Achiet le Grand	2.4.19		Left Englebelmer at 10 am and arrived at Achiet le Grand 1 pm. The weather is very severe very cold wind and snow, which is sure to increase the wastage in our horses.	
	3.4.19		Visited and inspected the animals of the 461 Company R.E. at Fichieres le Mans also the following units at same place 2/5 West Yorks 2/6 West Yorks 7part of the 116 & the 1st Section D.A.C. This has been so deaths in the last named during the night, as the result of exposure and bad condition. There are several thin animals in the 2/5 West Yorks, but milk general weather horses purse up 2/6 West Yorks and looking fairly well.	
	4.4.19		Proceeded to Ercheu & inspected horses of 311 Bde R.F.A. During the day & night of the 3rd inst there was severe frost & snow, which turned the roads & many around slippery. This Bde relieves the 310 Bde. Instructions were given to send all thin & debility cases not likely to stand this trying weather to M.V.S. Visited & inspected at Lignieres the 310 Bde horses, up to recently the animals of this Bde Kept condition fairly well, but now a good few are showing signs of debility. As they are kept two nights together and had work with no shelter, can hardly hope for improvement.	

Army Form C. 2118.

WAR DIARY
of A.D.V.S.
INTELLIGENCE SUMMARY.
62nd Division
(Erase heading not required.)

Instructions regarding War Diaries and Intelligence Summaries are contained in F.S. Regs., Part II. and the Staff Manual respectively. Title pages will be prepared in manuscript.

Place	Date	Hour	Summary of Events and Information	Remarks and references to Appendices
Achiet le Grand	5.4.17		Visited the horse lines of the D.A.C. near Bancourt. The animals of this unit are suffering in the same way as the Artillery from overwork & the bigger of the 2nd mal. seemed numerous death. Instructions have been given to evacuate all animals suffering stiffness or showing signs of it. Visited and inspected the animals of the MS. F.O.V.S.D. at Achiet le Petit. They are looking well. Had a visit from D.D.V.S and discussed the high percentage of mange in animals with causes.	
"	6.4.17		Visited the horse lines of 515 Company A.S.C. at Sapignies Inspected all the horses that have not out at work. Instructions were given to send several sick animals for evacuation. Visited inspected the horses of the 516, 537 & 538 Company's A.S.C. near Achiet le Grand. Found that the animals in these units show evidence of hard work, and no doubt the severe weather has caused them to suffer in condition. The animals in 516 Company are looking worse than the others. I think the stable management is bad might be improved. Visited the horse lines of the 460 T.M. Company R.E. at Achiet le Petit. Found the majority of the animals gone on their work, some showing to another section.	
"	7.4.17		Visited the horse lines of Divisional Signal Company. The animals in this unit are standing the severe strain of hard work & bad weather fairly well	

Army Form C. 2118.

WAR DIARY
of
INTELLIGENCE SUMMARY.
(Erase heading not required.)

Instructions regarding War Diaries and Intelligence Summaries are contained in F. S. Regs., Part II. and the Staff Manual respectively. Title pages will be prepared in manuscript.

A.D.V.S. 63rd Division

Place	Date	Hour	Summary of Events and Information	Remarks and references to Appendices
Achiet le Grand	7.4.17		Visited and inspected horse lines of ~19 Inf.? Eastern R.H.C at their lines Near Achiet le Grand a good few animals in mud. These units have been for a Considerable time to the line worn and severe weather. Visited and inspected the animals of the 186 Infantry Brigade at their lines Near Achiet le Grand. The animals of this Infantry Brigade have kept two troopy Trains and have not better than the Artillery.	
"	8.4.17		Visited inspected the animals of the 701 Machine Gun Company, stock of Achiet le Grand also 253rd Machine Gun Company at the Same area. Inspected the animals of 53rd Machine Gun Company at Ervillers. The animals of these units are looking well. Inspected at Ervillers the animals of 62 Bde R.F.A instructions from A.D.V.S to evacuate a number of debilitate animals. Visited reinspected at Ervillers 185th Infantry Brigade animals. The animals changing to the 11 Eastern R.H.C Shoeing of the 5/o Field Ambulance is animals of the 186th Field Amb The animals of the 186th Infantry Brigade are looking very well with one or two exceptions. Inspected animals of the Company R.E at Ervillers all looking fit.	
"	9.4.17		Visited reinspected the animals at the W.M.R. Mobile Veterinary Section at Mienvement for evacuation on the Rly. Inspected the animals of the 4th Section D.T.C near Mienvement. Stationary and in leathers is not quite as good as I might be not torgant, morainally with the other leathers	

T.134. Wt. W.708-776. 500000. 4/16. Sir J. C. & S.

Army Form C. 2118.

WAR DIARY
of
INTELLIGENCE SUMMARY.
(Erase heading not required.)

D.O.V.S.
62nd Division

Instructions regarding War Diaries and Intelligence Summaries are contained in F. S. Regs., Part II. and the Staff Manual respectively. Title pages will be prepared in manuscript.

Place	Date	Hour	Summary of Events and Information	Remarks and references to Appendices
Achiet le Grand	10.4.17		Visited the horse lines of the 30th Brigade at Boyigneux. The animals in nearly all the Batterys of this Brigade have lost flesh rapidly the last 8 or 10 days. The majority of animals have been doing an average trek of 10 mile per day for the past four days. There are a great many which appear to be very exhausted. Some have died in harness. Others have done in & has their incidents collapsed & died. The horses in D Battery are the worst. Visited & inspected the animals of No 1 Company R.E. at Boyigneux. There are looking fairly well. No animals suffering from debility have to be sent to M.V.S. for evacuation. Visited & inspected all the animals that were in at the horse lines Boyigneux of the 525- Company A.S.C. The hard work and severe weather is reducing many of these animals in condition. The Mobile Veterinary Section moved today from Miraumont to Achiet le Grand.	
"	11.4.17		Visited and inspected at the Boyigneux horse lines kept Achiet le Grand the animals of No 1 Section M.T.C. Visited & inspected what animals were in at the Boyigneux horse lines Kept Achiet le Grand of the following Companies A.S.C. 526. 527. 528. 529. 538. Several animals in 526 Company are becoming debilitated & are to be evacuated. The severe weather & hard work is causing a loss of condition in nearly all these animals. Owing to Motor Transport not being available it means nearly double work to A.S.C. horses.	

T2134. Wt. W708—776. 500000. 4/15. Sir J. C. & 8.

WAR DIARY
INTELLIGENCE SUMMARY

Army Form C. 2118.

A.D.V.S.
62nd Div.

Place	Date	Hour	Summary of Events and Information	Remarks and references to Appendices
Achiet le Grand	12.4.17		Visited & inspected animals for evacuation at the A.V. Section Achiet le Grand. The D.D.V.S. 5th Army called at this office and made enquiries as to wastage in animals, also evacuations & debilities cases. Visited & inspected the animals of the 1st, 2nd & 3rd Section D.R.S. at Bapaume.	
"	13.4.17		Visited and inspected the following animals at the horse lines Ervillers. 3rd Bde R.F.A. 460 & 461 Company R.E. and 185th Infantry Bde West of Ervillers. The horses in stall having a big percentage of wastage. Evacuations. The rest in these hand have been stopped during the past week. The Engineer units & Infantry animals are scrutinising the Shew fairly well. Visited the A.V. Section at Achiet le Grand, and inspected the animals of the Signal Company R.E.	
"	14.4.17		Visited and inspected the animals of the following units at Mory. 202, 208 & 213 Machine Gun Company's, 310th Brigade R.F.A. All the animals in the front these units are keeping condition fairly & there has been no casualties. There are still a number of Debility cases in the 310th Bde R.F.A. indications have been given to send these animals to A.V.S. for evacuation. Visited the Mobile Veterinary Section. A large number of animals are being sent in by the Cavalry units for evacuation.	
"	15.4.17		Visited and inspected animals at H(16R) M.V.S. Visited and inspected at Ervillers the animals of the 2/1 (6R) Field Ambulance. Visited & inspected animals of Divisional H.Qrs and the Divisional Signal Company R.E. at Achiet le Grand. The animals in nearly all these units are losing condition due to continuous hard work & severe weather	

WAR DIARY
of
INTELLIGENCE SUMMARY.
(Erase heading not required.)

Army Form C. 2118.

H.Q.V.S. 65th Division

Place	Date	Hour	Summary of Events and Information	Remarks and references to Appendices
Ashurst le Grand	16.4.17		Visited and inspected animals in the 2/1 (S.M.R.) M.V.S for evacuation on the 17th. Col Emma Cunningham V.D.M.S., S.A. Army called at this office to day in reference to the high percentage of Wastage in the Division caused by Debility and Exhaustion. he visited the horse lines of the 310th & 311th Brigade R.F.A. and had long conversation with several of the horse line officers. The problem discussed was if any measures could be adopted that would lessen the amount of Artillery horses the Veterinary Officers was sent into and shall manage and generally.	
"	17.4.17		Visited and inspected the animals of the following units at Ecrillers 185th Infantry Brigade 2/4 Yorks Lancs 7/5th K.O.Y.L.I of the 187th Brigade. The 460 & 461 Company R.E. The animals of these units are looking fairly well and are standing the hard work they have had better than the Artillery	
"	18.4.17		Visited & inspected at Ecrillers The animals of the 311th Brigade R.F.A. The 7/5(S.R.) Field Ambulance a few animals in the former are showing signs of Debility medications were given to hand on send to M.V.S for evacuation. The steamers went on telling on the animals of the latter unit. Visited & inspected the animals for evacuation in 2/1(S.R.) M.V.S. These: The animals in the 1st Section D.A.C. have become absorbed by the 310th &311th Brigades R.F.A.	
"	19.4.17		Visited and inspected at Tapighnies the animals of the 310th Bde R.F.A The 457th Company R.E. and 55s Company A.S.C. deemed the animals on Veterinary ask to send to M.V.S. Many of the R.E. and A.S.C. Company animals are foot of predating Debility owing owing to continues hard work	

Army Form C. 2118.

Instructions regarding War Diaries and Intelligence Summaries are contained in F. S. Regs., Part II. and the Staff Manual respectively. Title pages will be prepared in manuscript.

WAR DIARY
of
INTELLIGENCE SUMMARY.

F.A.F.S. 62nd Division

(Erase heading not required.)

Place	Date	Hour	Summary of Events and Information	Remarks and references to Appendices
Ablé le Grand	20.4.17		Visited and inspected the animals of the 2/1 West Field Ambulance at Ablé le Grand. a number of these animals are in a low condition particularly the heavy ones used for drawing the ambulances. they have been much overworked since the beginning of the clearances in consequence of the motor ambulances not being available. We hoped a rest will improve them, if not they must be evacuated. Visited and inspected the Horses and Mules of N° 7 & 2 Stations L.H.C. at Bethagnies. These animals are looking well generally speaking. Except for 30.4. and 9 there is no doubt if we have some good weather they will all improve in condition and appearance generally. Visited and inspected animals for evacuation in M.V.S. the majority of cases are Debility. Afterwards the section is greatly engaged in consequence of having to deal with evacuations from other units in the neighborhood. V3 58th Division Heavy Artillery. Cavalry Division 7.11th Division.	
"	21.4.17		Visited and inspected the animals of the 312 & M.T. Company at Gommecourt. Some of these animals have bad condition and are arrived in this country. Visited and inspected the Heavy Motors of the Horse Companys of the Divisional Train. Most the animals in these units have also the Heavy Coys and bad weather fairly well. These are a few in their condition in 336 & 337 Companys. Visited and inspected the animals of 460 & 461 Companys R.E at Ervillers and 457 & Company R.E at Logeignies with the exception of half a dozen animals in the latter all are looking well.	

Army Form C. 2118.

WAR DIARY
of
INTELLIGENCE SUMMARY.
(Erase heading not required.)

MOVS
60th Divisions

Instructions regarding War Diaries and Intelligence Summaries are contained in F. S. Regs., Part II. and the Staff Manual respectively. Title pages will be prepared in manuscript.

Place	Date	Hour	Summary of Events and Information	Remarks and references to Appendices
Behind the Lines	22.4.17		Visited and inspected animals of Mobile Veterinary Section. Visited Echellow & inspected animals of the 301st Brigade R.F.A. There is a noticeable improvement in that animals in a few days of holly dry & rest and good weather. Visited Echellow & inspected the animals of the 1/5 Field Ambulance & few of the heavy animals that were low in condition are gradually improving.	
	23.4.17		Inspected the animals of 301st Brigade R.F.A. at Napoynes. The majority in this brigade are showing signs of improvement and this is noticeable for by a percent of Rest and a few days sunshine. There is room for improvement in the horse of "D" Battery these animals seem to have suffered more on the march than those of the other Batteries of the Brigade. Proceeded to Marny & inspected the animals of the 3/3rd Inn. Company all looking fit and in forma condition. Suspected the 188th Infantry Brigade at Marny. Every care and attention appears to be given to these animals and at present are the best in the Division. Inspected the animals attached to 1/3 Field ambulance from 1/5 F.A. at Marny. one or two heavy draught are in poor condition as a result of over work.	
"	24.4.17		Visited and inspected the following animals at Echellow, all belonging to 188th Brigade. The 187th Brigade. The 1/05th Company R.E. The 1/06th Company R.E. The animals in the 183rd Infantry Brigade do not compare favourably with some of their founding Brigade. They are low in condition & more attention to grooming ought to be given.	

WAR DIARY of INTELLIGENCE SUMMARY.

Army Form C. 2118.

A.D.V.S.
62nd Division

Place	Date	Hour	Summary of Events and Information	Remarks and references to Appendices
Achiet le Grand	24.4.17		The animals of the HQ York and Lancs regiment a little more attention and were rather if possible in worse order. The C.O. concerning this matter. The animals of the 461 M.T. MT Coy R.E. are still looking thin particularly those that had to be shipped recently on account of Mange. The hopes good weather rest will improve the animals of this unit. Inspected the animals of the 457/4 Company R.E. at Ayuyneres. There is noticeable improvement in these since my last visit a few days. Inspected animals of 71 (WR) Field Ambulance at Achiet le Petit. There is an improvement in this lot. but they require a long period of Rest. as many the animals which have been returned by the H (WR) Field Ambulance look as if it has been worked till dropped at Achiet le Grand horses of the 2/3 W. Field Ambulance all looking well. Visited and inspected animals at H(WR) Mobile Veterinary Section	
"	25.4.17		Visited the Waffen Lines at Lapignies of the 308 Brigade R.F.A. and inspected the animals. Fans B. Batteries are looking well and have much improved this past week. C and D Batteries animals are making little progress. These animals have the appearance of having been greatly over worked and in my opinion it will take a long period of Rest the best attention and good weather to make them fit. Visited inspected the animals of Divisional Head Quarters & M.T. at Achiet le Grand	

WAR DIARY
of
INTELLIGENCE SUMMARY.

Army Form C. 2118.

A.D.T.S. 63rd Division

(Erase heading not required.)

Instructions regarding War Diaries and Intelligence Summaries are contained in F.S. Regs., Part II. and the Staff Manual respectively. Title pages will be prepared in manuscript.

Place	Date	Hour	Summary of Events and Information	Remarks and references to Appendices
Hebuterne to Grand Serre			Visited and inspected the animals of the following units at Ecoivres Viz 31st Brigade R.F.A. the 187th Infantry Brigade 2/s Field Ambulance 461st Company, 31st Brigade Machine Gun Company. There are still a few animals in low condition in 10 Battery 31st R.F.A. But generally speaking there is an improvement. The rest and good weather of the past week has so improved the condition of the animals of A B & C Batteries that they will now be able to do reasonable work. There is also an improved condition in the animals of the 461st Company R.E. but they still require rest & good rations. Visited the M.T. at Hebuterne to Grand. Sergeant Blundell reported for duty in place of Sergeant Shannon. T.D.C. now posted to 6 by 6 Howitzer Bde. Visited and inspected animals in M.T. at Hebuterne to Grand. Visited transport of the troops being Belgian animals of Nos 1 7 & 1/3 Sections 10.A.C. there are looking in fair condition particularly No. 1 Section. Inspected the animals of the 71 (W.R.) Field Ambulance at Belogues. That are improving but still require rest and general attention. Inspected animals of the 34 Squad: Forts at Belogues all looking fit. Inspected the horse master of 5 & 9 Company, Harnessed Trans are an improvement with one or two exceptions they are looking well. Inspected at Hebuterne to Grand the animals of the Divisional Signal Company. These are going on fairly well. Inspected animals of C and D Batteries 312nd Bde at Lagnicourt. Those in D Battery are improving. There are still many thin horses in the Battery	
	27.4.17			

T2134. Wt. W708 - 776. 500090. 4/15. Sir J. C. & S.

WAR DIARY of INTELLIGENCE SUMMARY

Army Form C. 2118.

K.O.R.,
62nd Division

Place	Date	Hour	Summary of Events and Information	Remarks and references to Appendices
Achiet le Grand	29.11.17		Inspected the animals of the following Company. Divisional Train at the Wagon Lines 356", 357" & 358" the horses in the latter are looking fat indeed. In the 357" Company there is an improvement. In the 356" Company the animals have an unthrifty appearance and look as if they required more attention. Inspected the animals of the following units at Gomiecourt. Hq. 313" Machine Gun Company, Head Quarters of the 185" Infantry Brigade & the Hq. West Yorks. The Machine Gun mules are not in good condition so on my last visit. At present they are doing a good deal of work.	
"	29.11.17		Visited and inspected the animals of the following units at Neuf Wagon Lines near Ervillers C.R.D. Battery 313 Brigade R.F.A. 461 Company R.E. 208" Machine Gun Company. The lines Iance 7th K.O.Y.L.I. 96 & Hq. West Yorks. 2/5 K.O.Y.L.I. and 2/5 Yorks & Lancs. The mobile veterinary section 461 Company R.E. The animals in other units look fairly well except the 208" M.G. Company which have gone off in condition. I am of the opinion the continuous engagement in this unit is not good. Some cases of suspect mange in M.V.S. Many animals in D Battery 313 Bde as lousy and are clipped out are spotted giving the appearance of mange. All animals in this Battery are being clipped and dressed as a precautionary measure.	
"	30.11.17		Visited Irregularer animals at A.D.V.S. Station. Visited and inspected D Battery animals 313 Bde all clipped animals are being dressed. Attended Conference held by D.A.V.S. 5th Army at 58 Division Head Quarters. Continued	

Army Form C. 2118.

WAR DIARY

of

A.D.V.S.

INTELLIGENCE SUMMARY.

62nd Division

(Erase heading not required.)

Instructions regarding War Diaries and Intelligence Summaries are contained in F.S. Regs., Part II. and the Staff Manual respectively. Title pages will be prepared in manuscript.

Place	Date	Hour	Summary of Events and Information	Remarks and references to Appendices
Achiet le Grand	21.11.17	Continued	and discussed the formation of a Corps Mobile Veterinary Section. Three men are to be supplied by the Mobile A.V.S. to form part of personnel, a part of the equipment is also to be handed over. If the Division leaves 5th Corps men will be returned & equipment. Capt Brown AVC granted 10 days leave.	

J F Neill Major AVS
A.D.V.S. 62nd Division

Original

Confidential
Vol 5

War Diary
of
ADVS 62nd Division

FROM: 1-5-17
TO: 31-5-17

Volume 5

Army Form C. 2118.

WAR DIARY
of
INTELLIGENCE SUMMARY.
(Erase heading not required.)

M.O.R.S.
61st Division

Instructions regarding War Diaries and Intelligence Summaries are contained in F.S. Regs., Part II. and the Staff Manual respectively. Title pages will be prepared in manuscript.

Place	Date	Hour	Summary of Events and Information	Remarks and references to Appendices
Field &c General	1.5.17		Inspected the animals of the 210th Brigade R.F.A. and the Wagon lines. Many of the animals are very mangy & medication have been given to have them clipped and dressed. The remount Officer particularly to C. & D Batteries. If a little more attention are given to grooming the state of things could not occur. Visited respecting the animals of C and D Batteries 31st Bde R.F.A. a number of animals that were clipped in the other Battery on account of mangy or account of soreness on further inspection, shew symptoms of mange. Every effort is being made to control the further spread and stamp out the disease. Visited respecting animals 31(H.&R) Bde, 1.T.S. & the 2/1 (1st) Field Ambulance.	
"	5.5.17		Inspected the animals of the 213th & 201st Machine Gun Companies (near Berry). The former required a little more attention in grooming medication, from to chip and kennel. The latter a good lot - all well cared. Inspected the animals of the 186th Infantry Brigade. Horses are losing their attention in the Division. Visited and inspected at Boyhens the animals of 1/5 & 2 Section D.A.C. This is an improvement on those. General mark of long last inspection of lines. There are to be clipped. Inspected at Boyhens the animals of the 457 & 458 Company R.E. & these have a marked improvement	
"	8.5.17		Visited and inspected the animals of the following units in and around Emiller 2/7th, 2/8th, 2/6th Infantry Bde, 466 Company R.E. 2/5 & 2/4 West Yorks & 3/1 Brigade R.F.A. on further inspection of the animals of animals transport drawn in D.3057	

Army Form C. 2118.

WAR DIARY
of
INTELLIGENCE SUMMARY.

A.D.V.S.
6th Division

(Erase heading not required.)

Instructions regarding War Diaries and Intelligence Summaries are contained in F. S. Regs., Part II. and the Staff Manual respectively. Title pages will be prepared in manuscript.

Place	Date	Hour	Summary of Events and Information	Remarks and references to Appendices
Achiet le Grand	3.5.17		Visited the post of operations formed after clipping in order to test clippings have been tested off of the animals being passed forward. Generally the animals are improving in weakly many cases.	
"	4.5.17		Visited and inspected the animals of the 43 Field Ambulance near Achiet le Grand. They are looking in fit condition. Visited and inspected the animals of the 536, 537, & 538 (Company) Divisional Train at their lines near Gomiecourt Rd. The animals of 536 Company also appear in satisfactory condition, but as of anything slightly improved since my last visit. 538 Company are very poor 537 rapidly improving. Had the A.V.S. Inspectors remount that arrived from Albepuille. Visited remounts at Behagnies. The animals of the 48 (Hvy) Yorks and 2/1 Field Ambulance the head Yorks were very fair but will improve. The draught animals in the Field Ambulance are in a low condition and have not recovered from the severe hours off a few weeks back. Visited and inspected at Ervillers No v D Batteries 3rd R Bde. had of the animals are clipping out and look smart, but I think they are slow for the moment from transit. This remount applies to C Battery. Visited remounts at Behagnies 17 v Section 10.S.A.C. The animals are looking fairly fit. Onward draw of Battenes are being clipped out, and dressed. Visited the R.V.S.	JRn

Army Form C. 2118.

A.D.V.S.
62nd Division

WAR DIARY
of
INTELLIGENCE SUMMARY.
(Erase heading not required.)

Place	Date	Hour	Summary of Events and Information	Remarks and references to Appendices
Achiet le Grand	6.5.19		Visited and inspected the animals of 310th Brigade R.F.A. horse lines. The condition & appearance generally of 6 & 10 Batteries is not good. Their Gears, to be inspected, grooming & Shoes more attention. Stores to from to Steenwerjck. A & B Batteries are in much better condition & there are fair Visitors: Inspected draught animals of 338 Company Divisional Train. They are looking well & the Boot Treatment over has repeatedly improving. Visited the M.V.S.	
"	7.5.19		Visited Inspected animals of the 308th Machine Gun Company Horse lines. There are still a few in thin and in a thin condition. The appearance of the animals generally from one the improvement of last in horse mastership. Inspected the animals of the York and Lanes at Ervillers hese appeared to be some improvement on this week. Fuel. There is still room for more. Inspected animals of the N. York Lanes. There are fairly good. Inspected animals of 466th Company R.E. all lost in foot condition. Horse lines Visited the Mayor Linnes of 351st Company R.E. and inspected animals. Notice a great improvement in the lot. Visited inspected the animals of 311th Brigade R.F.A. The condition of the animals in this Brigade is fairly good. There are still a number suffering from Lice. These are being clipped & dressed Wrote Asst Quartie stating the Sand in Achiel le Grand was unfit for horse drinking water.	
"	8.5.19		Visited inspected animals in A.V. Spear & Evacuation.	

WAR DIARY
INTELLIGENCE SUMMARY.
(Erase heading not required.)

Army Form C. 2118.

F.O.V.S.
63rd Division.

Place	Date	Hour	Summary of Events and Information	Remarks and references to Appendices
Abbele de Fms	Continued 8.5.17		Visited & inspected the animals of Divisional Signal Company. These have much improved — the past week. Visited & inspected the animals of no.1 Company R.E. There is decided improvement on the animals of this unit. Inspected at Boury the animals of the 213th Machine Gun Company. These animals need more for improvement in that unit. There are many of them thin and do not appear well groomed.	
"	9.5.17		Visited and inspected at the Beggar Farm loss of lines the animals of the 189th Brigade R.F.A with the exception of the animals in D Battery all seem to be improving in condition. A great number in each Battery are loosing and when clipped appear very patchy but so far I see none with mange. Visited and inspected the animals of 213th M. Gun Comp.y near there these are looking fairly well. Attended at Entrées transportation on the horses stig, Gun Respirators are here & fire same in position.	
"	10.5.17		Visited and inspected the animals of the N.B. and Coy No. at Tournelles. there is not much improvement in some of these probably due to their being in possession of sickness arrangement. Inspected at Entrées the animals of the following Units, all the 168th Infantry Brigade, the 189th Infantry Brigade, 174 T.C.H.S. and 188th Machine Gun Company. The animals of the Infantry Brigades are looking fairly well particularly the 188th. The animals in the 189th M.G. Regiment a little more attention should be bestowed upon se of the unit. The bitts or no knowledge of this dution.	

Army Form C. 2118.

WAR DIARY
of
INTELLIGENCE SUMMARY.
(Erase heading not required.)

A.V.T.S. 63rd Division

Instructions regarding War Diaries and Intelligence Summaries are contained in F. S. Regs., Part II. and the Staff Manual respectively. Title pages will be prepared in manuscript.

Place	Date	Hour	Summary of Events and Information	Remarks and references to Appendices
Mobile to France	11.5.17		Visited and inspected the Major Lines Bologne the animals of Mar & M's Sections D.A.C. The animals in both Sections are looking fairly fit, particularly M's. Visites and inspected the animals of 526, 527 and 558 Company's of Divisional Train. This is a marked improvement in 526 & 527 Company's animals. Visited and inspected animals in Mobile Vety Section.	
"	12.5.17		Visited and inspected the animals of the 313th Brigade R.F.A. the animals are all improving, but a little more attention to grooming is necessary. Also has reference more particularly to C Battery. Visited and inspected animals of the 331 Company Div Train at Van Meester Lines. Not about 30 replaces all are looking well improving in condition.	
"	13.5.17		Capt Brown A.V.C. reported for duty after 10 days leave. Visited and inspected animals of 326th Brigade R.F.A. There is an improvement in all the animals, but those of D Battery are very slow. They are either being over-horsed or not getting proper attention. Shoe points and 2 let bygone lines in several occasions that in my opinion they require more attention. Visited and inspected animals of 313 Th G Company all are looking in good condition, a few lame and regular shopping. Visited Hospital animals on A.V. 31. Wood Line.	
"	14.5.17		Visited and inspected the animals of the 46, 47, 78, 4 Casualties also the 203rd Av. G. Company hospitals animals.	
"	15.5.17		The 3H 6 R's Mobile Veterinary Section was visited by the M.D.V.S. accompanied by Major N. Jones A.V.C.	KN

WAR DIARY
INTELLIGENCE SUMMARY

(Erase heading not required.)

Army Form C. 2118.

A.D.V.S.
62nd Division

Instructions regarding War Diaries and Intelligence Summaries are contained in F.S. Regs., Part II. and the Staff Manual respectively. Title pages will be prepared in manuscript.

Place	Date	Hour	Summary of Events and Information	Remarks and references to Appendices
Achiet le Grand	13.5.17	Continued	Capt. Abson of M.V.S. was present during the visit. Visited and inspected the animals of the following units of Divisional and Artillery and neighbourhood, Viz: 460, 461 Company R.E., the 186th & 187th Infantry Brigade, the 208th & 213th Machine Gun Company's. There is an improvement in the condition of the animals generally with the exception of the 74 Divn of Wellington; and 208th Machine Gun Company. There is an indication since the intermixing of Greys. It is a little Grooming as possible. Inspected the animals at the M.V.S.	
"	14.5.17		Visited and inspected the animals of 310th Brigade R.F.A. Near Irery. A.T.B. battery animals are looking fairly well. but those of C.D. are unsatisfactory still although showing a slight improvement. The Grooming in the latter two batteries requires more attention. Visited and inspected the animals of C D Battries 313th Brigade. There is an improvement in D Battery Slightly so in C. With the exception of a few animals there seems to be a lack of knowledge in Stable management is not enough hand brushes to Grooming. Visited and inspected animals in Mr. V.S.	
"	15.5.17		Visited inspected at Bapaume 85 remounts consisting of 70 L.D. for the Artillery 15 H.D. for Bus. train. Visits and inspected at Haff[?] Jnce the animals of 761.78 sections D.A.C. Inspected at the Waggon Lines the animals of 56s Company R.E.C.	

Original

Army Form C. 2118.

WAR DIARY
of
A.D.V.S.
63rd Division
INTELLIGENCE SUMMARY
(Erase heading not required.)

Instructions regarding War Diaries and Intelligence Summaries are contained in F. S. Regs., Part II. and the Staff Manual respectively. Title pages will be prepared in manuscript.

Place	Date	Hour	Summary of Events and Information	Remarks and references to Appendices
Field G. Shows	19.5.17		Visited and inspected the animals of the 188th Infantry Brigade and Surveillon, also the 315th Machine Gun Company & the 160th Field Ambulance. Many of the animals in the latter unit are thin and unthrifty and required more attention as regards feeding. Also Major Gregory will inspect them. Visited & inspected animals of Divisional Signal Company at Aitol. A. Found that they were looking fairly well. Inspected animals in Mobile Veterinary Section.	
"	19.5.17		Visited & inspected the animals of the 315th Brigade R.F.A. BC & D Batteries are improving but I think there is a falling off in condition of A Battery animals. The standings of this unit in very insanitary & I have asked that they be moved into more healthy surroundings if possible. Visited and inspected animals in M.V.S.	
			J. O'Neill Major A.V.C. A.D.V.S. 63rd Div	
"	20.5.17		A.D.V.S. departed on leave to England; Capt Alison A.V.C. took over the duties during his absence. Paid a visit to Mory & inspected all the animals of the 310th Bde R.F.A. Instructed O.C. B.ty to send his animals into M.V.S. & one from A. Bty. Also Inspected animals of Div. H.Q. Gps & H.dqrs R.F.A. 63rd Div.	
"	21.5.17		Visited & inspected animals of 156th Infantry Bde; 2/1 & 2/3 W. Lanc Field Ambulances. The hy Bde. animals are not quite in the condition which they ought to be & several have been put on separate	(P.W.)

T.134. Wt. W708-773. 50000. 4/15. Sir J. C. & S.

Army Form C. 2118.

WAR DIARY
or
INTELLIGENCE SUMMARY.
(Erase heading not required.)

A.528
62nd Division

Place	Date	Hour	Summary of Events and Information	Remarks and references to Appendices
Robert le Grand (continued)	22.5.17		Since the end of the week there have been special attention. The 3rd Field Amb. animals are very much improved. The 213th Field Amb. are satisfactory. Inspected animals of 213th Machine Gun Corps. Several thin animals have been reported for special attention.	
"	22.5.17		Visited Repairers inspected animals being detained. Bates Nitro Groin & R.H. Inspected animals in M.V.S. for evacuation.	
"	23.5.17		Visited 312th Batt. R.F.A. There is still a number of animals on the line order to improvement but as before. Visited the 185th Infantry Bde, these animals are certainly to make satisfactory progress. Visited 2/2 Field Ambulance, these animals are much improved. Visited 206th Machine Gun Corps, there is a marked improvement in these animals.	
"	24.5.17		Visited 201st Machine Gun Battalion, animals in good condition. Visited 460 & 462 animals in food condition. 461 Coy R.E. animals improving. 457 Coy R.E. animals improving but still not satisfactory. the 1299 inspected for evacuation to this Service. Visited 2/3rd York & Lancs Animals, still several these animals but improving. Visited 2/4th York & Lancs Animals, they are improving. Visited 2/4 K.O.Y.L.I. Regt. several poor animals, not up to the second standard of the Bde.	
"	25.5.17		Visited 310th Batt. R.F.A. inspecting animals, steady improvement previously. The three are making satisfactory progress. Inspected Brencoral Hill animals, condition satisfactory.	

WAR DIARY or INTELLIGENCE SUMMARY

Army Form C. 2118.

ADS 62nd Division

Place	Date	Hour	Summary of Events and Information	Remarks and references to Appendices
Achiet le Grand (continued)	24.5.17		Visited R.A.M.C. arrivals satisfactory. Inspected arrivals of Mobile Veterinary Section for evacuation.	
"	26.5.17		Inspected arrivals of sick animals, hot water in foot bath - no cases are improving. Visited Mobile Veterinary Section. Visited horses and signals posts. R.A. H.Q. Am. T. Examined sick of 60 animals.	
"	27.5.17		Visited remounts of 312th Bde R.F.A. Condition of all animals improved, the several in the firm state. Three cases lame - sent into M.V.S. Visited 62nd Div Signal Coy. The animals much improved & are generally satisfactory. Several cases of remounts not yet quite fit for line from the cents.	
"	29.5.17		Visited 326 Coy, 527 Coy, & 52889 A.S.C. inspected all animals. The condition is satisfactory. Several animals in 329 Coy require fuller further improvement. Visited M.V.S. Inspected animals for evacuation. Visited R.A. + Sect. Heads of animals.	
"	30.5.17		Visited 312 K. Bde R.F.A. all animals improved. Visited 525 Coy A.S.C. animals generally in fair condition. Visit R.A. + Sect. H.Qrs animals. Inspected arrivals in M.V.S. for evacuation.	

P. Walker Captain
For A.D.V.S. 62nd Division

1) Original Vol 6

Confidential
War Diary
of
A.D.V.S. - 62nd Division

From 1st June 17. To 30th June 17

Volume VI.

Original

Army Form C. 2118.

WAR DIARY
OF
INTELLIGENCE SUMMARY.
(Erase heading not required.)

J.M.V.S.
63rd Division

Instructions regarding War Diaries and Intelligence Summaries are contained in F.S. Regs., Part II. and the Staff Manual respectively. Title pages will be prepared in manuscript.

Place	Date	Hour	Summary of Events and Information	Remarks and references to Appendices
Achiet le Grand	1.6.19		Returned from leave and resumed duty. Visited vinspected the animals in Mobile Veterinary Section. Inspected animals of Divisional Head Quarters.	
"	2.6.19		Visited and inspected animals of the 3rd Bde R.H.A. There is a marked improvement in the condition of the animals of this Brigade, but there is a few them even in each of the Batteries. Visited vinspected the animals of No.1 & No.2 Stations 10,9,0 to 1 Section Shows much improvement. Visited vinspected remounts at Expense Station.	
"	3.6.19		Visited and inspected the animals of the 187th Infantry Brigade, animals looking fairly well. There is still room for improvement in 2/15 K.O.Y.L.I. Inspected animals of the 208th Machine Gun Company. These animals are much improved. Visited and inspected the animals of the 186th Infantry Brigade at Behut le Petit. This is a fair Brigade. Inspected the animals of the No.91 Company R.E. Much improved in condition. Visited vinspected animals in No.1.18	
"	4.6.19		Visited and inspected the animals of 3rd A Brigade R.H.A. near Aerg. D Battery animals and horses impressed. A & B are good. C improved but require more attention in grooming. Visited vinspected animals of the 211 Machine Gun Company at Achiet le Grand, a very food unit. Inspected animals of 526, 534 & 536 Companies (continued) L.S.B.

WAR DIARY
or
INTELLIGENCE SUMMARY.   F.A.V.S.
2nd Division

Army Form C. 2118.

Place	Date	Hour	Summary of Events and Information	Remarks and references to Appendices
Aubigny sur Nerre				
	4.6.17		Arrival of horses. The animals of the 55th Company show a marked improvement in condition and formerly 15 y Company is doing fairly well. 55th Company good. Under M.F.S.	
	5.6.17		Paid a surprise visit to the 183rd Infantry Brigade near Epineuse. The animals of the Brigade show not improvement of any sort on the horses in the rear. Satisfactory reports at arrive. Place and had visited the animals of the 113rd Machine Gun Company. There is room for much improvement in this unit in the way of stable management. Visits and inspected at Belognies the animals of the following units. 13 & 15 Field Ambulance, 110 Company R.E. and 55N Company. Received them the former as I would like, as regards to foot. H.R.F. Company not progressing as much as I would like, as regards condition. The A.N.C. requires a little more attention in grooming.	
	6.6.17		Visited inspected at Epineuse the 66 Companys R.E. animals and better kept. Hypoolic has improved, the animals of the 113 Field Ambulance I have visited twice the first of the 9 Field Ambulance. This is my first movement on the latter. Visits impaired at Noyen Gran's has improved. The animals of 6th Brigade FAD speaking generally, they are looking fairly well, but they are still suffering from many thousand pasterns. J.B.D. Batterson	

WAR DIARY
INTELLIGENCE SUMMARY.

Army Form C. 2118.

of J.W.T. Glover
62nd Division

Place	Date	Hour	Summary of Events and Information	Remarks and references to Appendices
Behind the Lines	7.6.17		Visited and inspected the armourers of the 8th Infantry Brigade at Magen Cines near Bihucourt. The armourer of the following units shewed little improvement in cleaning; that their is no attention to the use of fresh moisture to leave of proper attention. 4th Y & Y.C. 208th Machine Gun Company and the two Lewis of the K.O.Y.L.I. the other to be inspected. The armourer of the Lewis Guns L.H.C. at Chépinoirs. There are twenty-five Lewis guns, most in a hundred	
"	8.6.17		Visited and inspected armourers of the 30th Brigade R.F.A. near Mory. Host in a hundred improvement in the condition of their armourers, Particularly in C & D Batteries.	
"	9.6.17		Visited and inspected the armourers of the 186th Infantry Brigade at Adinfer le Petit. The condition of the armourers are fair, except 4/5th Duke of Wellington's that required more care and attention in fitting. Visited and inspected the armourers of the Divisional Signal Company at Adinfer le Grand. The condition of their armourers is satisfactory. Visited inspected the armourers of the following units in & about Gomiecourt. 18 460 Company R.E. 2/3 D.L.I. Ambulance 208 & Machine Gun Company and the 185th Infantry Brigade also armourers in M.D.S.	
"	10.6.17		Capt Alson left for 10 days leave in England.	
"	11.6.17		Visited and inspected the armourers of the 17/21 Field Ambulance, 2/5 King's Wellingtons, 218 Machine Gun Company Brigade Ambulance, 102 Company R.E. and Hdqtrs. Div. I think. No orders to all Companies not Company not exceed one journal at back of State management. As Rifles are not satisfactory.	

JWG

WAR DIARY
of
INTELLIGENCE SUMMARY.
(Erase heading not required.)

Army Form C. 2118.

F.M 15
61st Division

Place	Date	Hour	Summary of Events and Information	Remarks and references to Appendices
Schribcourt	12.6.17		Visited and inspected animals of the 183rd Infantry Brigade and reported on their condition to Divisional Head Quarters. (D Barrel) Visited Bauve and inspected the following animals of returns (a) C D horses 30 L D mules 3 charges and 2 Ponies. Visited and inspected the animals of (b) and 2 sections D.A.C. Generally speaking these are looking satisfactory. Visited and inspected animals at H.Q & 67th Mobile Veterinary Section for evacuation	
"	13.6.17		Visited and inspected animals of the 3rd ? Brigade R.F.A. The condition of the animals in A & D Batteries so far as those of B Battery not so good, they seem to require more attention than they are receiving these pointed this out to O.C. Found some of Specialis Section Horses in E Battery ans to be in Battery. Visited and inspected animals in M.T.S.	
"	14.6.17		Visited and inspected the animals of 302nd Brigade R.F.A. There is marked improvement in C & D Batteries H.Q.B. three in hand better condition than the latter two a month or 3 weeks ago but at present are not so good. Inspected 183rd Company R.E Animals at Hargea Wood troop transport looking fatter. Inspected animals for evacuation in M.T.S	
"	15.6.17		Visited and inspected animals of Divisional Signal Company, all looking well. Visited and inspected animals in Mobile Veterinary Section. Held a meeting of Veterinary officers	

WAR DIARY or INTELLIGENCE SUMMARY

Army Form C. 2118.

H.Q.V.S. 63rd Division

Place	Date	Hour	Summary of Events and Information	Remarks and references to Appendices
Aubigny	16.6.17		Capt. Robert L. Evans moved to Robert L. Pret. Visits and inspects the animals of the 31st Fld. Ambulance. There has been improvement. Inspects the animals of the 409th Coy R.E. No further cases of Mange in this unit.	
"	17.6.17		Visits and inspects animals of the following units. No. 755 M.T. Battalion Corps of Washington. Visits and inspects animals of the 2/3 Machine Gun Company at Robert L. Pret. The 188th Infantry Bgd. & 212 Machine Gun Company and 254 Company Divisional Train near Ecurie. There is no improvement in the animals of 213 M.G.C on no (?) Cond(?). The animals of 213 M.G.C are in such condition as they might be brought to this mark. The animals of 213 M.G.C on no improving. The animals of 213 M.G.C on no improving. The Mobile Veterinary Section moves from Robert L. Evans to Robert L. Pret.	
"	18.6.17		Visits and inspects animals of the 311th Brigade R.F.A. at Aujaine. Any remarks on this Brigade and the same as on the 16th inst. Inspects the animals of the 194th Infantry Brigade. There is an improvement in two Brigade particularly the 107th M.S.C.	
"	19.6.17		Visits Mobile Veterinary Station and inspects animals for Evacuation. Visits and inspects animals of the 315th Brigade R.F.A. at Hapgen. Have been many C and D Battery animals have improved much. A and B Battery have slightly gone off.	

R.L.B.

WAR DIARY or INTELLIGENCE SUMMARY.

Army Form C. 2118.

A.V.R.S., 63rd Division

Place	Date	Hour	Summary of Events and Information	Remarks and references to Appendices
Behind la Cité	20.6.17		Tents and inspected the animals of 189th Coy R.E. all looking satisfactory. Inspected the animals of the 76th H.B.I. Field Ambulance all looking well brought 3 mules to Rest a week. Inspected animals of N°1, 2 & 3 Sections D.T.C. There are a few their animals in N°1 and 2 Sections otherwise all looking in fair condition. Inspected animals of 58th Company Divisional Train. These are doing well. Trade 24 H.R. to I Section	
"	21.6.17		Trade and inspected the animals of the 23 Field Ambulance, the 106th Company R.E., the 536 and 528 Horsedrawn Divisional Train. The animals for inspection in Mobile Veterinary Section are animals that Quarters are unsuitable to assemble in open. Company animals are looking well, and those of the Field Ambulance and Company R.E. are in good condition. Captain Pelham, ATC, O.C. F.M.S.B. M.V.S reported for duty on return from leave	
"	22.6.17		Captain Croft, ATC, acting O.C. M.V.S returned to his unit on arrival of Capt. Pelham from leave. Had a meeting of Veterinary Officers of the Division and discussed procedures to have a Sub-for-indulcemts by sand attendance at Rehepural and an interview with new A.D.V.S. 3rd Corps	
"	23.6.17		The A.D.V.S. Capt. Angus, inspected the following lines in which classes of management were found improving from A.V.A. 76 and HQ 1st Coy of inf division and 2 HQ Companies 68 Infantry Brigade. No further action was taken. Ordered S. Remounts No. 670 E	E.S.M.

Army Form C. 2118.

WAR DIARY
or
INTELLIGENCE SUMMARY.
(Erase heading not required.)

Instructions regarding War Diaries and Intelligence Summaries are contained in F. S. Regs., Part II. and the Staff Manual respectively. Title pages will be prepared in manuscript.

K.D.V.S., 62nd Division

Place	Date	Hour	Summary of Events and Information	Remarks and references to Appendices
Field, etc.	24.6.17		Visited and inspected animals of Divisional Signal Company and 313th Machine Gun Company at Achiet le Petit, animals on these posts are looking well. Visited and inspected one pr. K.D.V.S. in new area.	
"	25.6.17		Visited the hopper lines of 312 Bde R.F.A. at their new location. Visited and inspected 6 A.V.S. animals for evacuation. Joined in Company with Lt. A.D.V.S. of 2nd Corps the Brf Infantry Brigade transport lines. An inspection was made by A.D.V.S. of all the animals in the Brigade. Visited and inspected animals of the 2/1st 2/3 Field Ambulances also under 236, 237 & 238 Companies of Divisional Train.	
"	26.6.17		Accompanied the A.D.V.S. V. Corps in the inspection of the animals at 30th Brigade R.F.A. Properly animals in 3/1(W.R.) Mobile Veterinary Section. Inspected Head Quarters animals. Sergt. Blundell A.V.C. attached to 187th Infantry Brigade joins on leave.	
"	27.6.17		Visited and inspected animals of the 306th Brigade R.F.A. Animals in Batteries A & B have gone down in condition, those in C & D are much improved and are now better than A & B. Visited and inspected animals in M.V. Section. O.A.C. These are looking well. Visited the M.V.S.	
"	28.6.17		Visited and inspected the animals of the following units located near Hermencourt viz:- Company R.E. No. 457 Section 62.D.S. 185 and 186 Infantry Brigades and the animals in M.V.S.	

T1134. Wt. W708—776. 500000. 4/15. Sir J. C. & S.

WAR DIARY
or
INTELLIGENCE SUMMARY.

Army Form C. 2118.

D.A.D.V.S. by ... [illegible]

(Erase heading not required.)

Place	Date	Hour	Summary of Events and Information	Remarks and references to Appendices
Movement Commands	29.6.17		Moved from Abbeville Rest to the Remount Camp and reported to the Officer in Charge Remounts.	
			The troops returning later from Abbeville to London. D.K. Stanton Shestoff.	
			Received wire from General Head Quarters instructing Capt. Shee O.C. 2/Her D.M.V.S to proceed to 3rd Division on his appointment a D.A.D.V.S. Visited and inspected the animals	
	30.6.17		in the "C" company of Remount team. Visited B.V.S.	
			Visited Buchicourt, and 10.0 am interview with A.D.V.S 3rd Corps with reference to filling	
			the vacancy in B.V.S caused by transfer of Capt. Ahern to V.H.	

B.M.

B. Neill
Major D.V.S
O.I.C. O.V. Unit No...

Original

Vol 7

Confidential

War Diary
of
A.A.& Q.M.G 62nd Division

From 1~7~17   To 31~7~17

Vol. VII

Original

WAR DIARY
or
INTELLIGENCE SUMMARY.
(Erase heading not required.)

Army Form C. 2118.

A.D.M.S.
63rd Division

Place	Date	Hour	Summary of Events and Information	Remarks and references to Appendices
Hennencourt	1.7.17		Captain Moore R.A.M.C. left the Division on his appointment as D.A.D.M.S. 5th Division. Visited and inspected animals of the 2nd & 3rd Dragoon R.A.M.C. 3rd, 4th and 5th Field Ambulances and the M.D.S. Had a report of the D.A.D.S. Corps who showed he was awaiting Capt R.H. Gratt A.V.C. new Joined for A.D. duties M.T.S.	
	2.7.17		Visited & inspected the animals in M/S for remounts. Inspected animals of the 106 Res. M.G. Machine Gun Company, B Battery, 315th Bty R.F.A. the M.T R.O.Y.L.I. & the V.T.C.	
	3.7.17		Inspected the animals of the 188th & 189th Infantry Brigades and 1st Machine Gun Co. Visited the M.T. Sectors. Inspected the animals of the 3rd Brigade R.F.A. 4 guns D Battery 30th A Bde R.F.A. and 213th Machine Gun Company.	
	4.7.17		Visited and inspected the animals of the Divisional Signal Company also M.T. Sectors.	
	5.7.17		Visited Supreme & Inspected remounts on arrival. Visited the Mobile Veterinary Section. Inspected the animals of N°s 1, 2 & 3 Sections D.A.C. and 555th Company Divisional Train. Had a meeting of V.O. of the Division. Capt Gratt appointed O.C. M(V.S.) M.T.S.	
	6.7.17		Visited M.D.O.R. M.V.S. the 2/1 and 2/3 (W.R) Field Ambulances and the 460th M.T. of Company's R.E. The animals of the 2/1 Field Ambulance are not looking quite so well as they did 10 day's ago. The animals in the other units are very satisfactory.	

J.B.K.

Original

Army Form C. 2118.

WAR DIARY
or
INTELLIGENCE SUMMARY.
(Erase heading not required.)

A.D.V.S. 63rd Division

Instructions regarding War Diaries and Intelligence Summaries are contained in F. S. Regs., Part II. and the Staff Manual respectively. Title pages will be prepared in manuscript.

Place	Date	Hour	Summary of Events and Information	Remarks and references to Appendices
Commander	7.7.17		The Division was for another area. The Division was come into 6th Corps. Visited and inspected the animals of the 293rd Brigade R.F.A. Army Corps. This animal was attached to the Division. Most of the animals are in bad condition except 3 R.C. which are good.	
"	8.7.17		Visited and inspected the animals in 336th, 537th and 338th Company Divisional Train	
"	9.7.17		Visited and inspected animals in H.Q.R.H. A.V.S. Inspected animals of the 2nd Brigade R.G.A. sick and had an interview with A.D.V.S. 6 Corps.	
"	10.7.17		Visited and inspected animals of the 3rd Brigade R.F.A., The 223rd Machine Gun Company the R.E. and 1/6 Infantry Brigade. All belonging to this Division.	
"	11.7.17		Visited and inspected the animals of the Q.M.G. and H.Q.R.E. Mobile Veterinary Section	
"	12.7.17		Visited and inspected the animals in the following units. H(63rd) Bty R.E. 127th Infantry Brigade 157th Company R.E. The 308th, 313th and 333rd Machine Gun Company.	
"	13.7.17		Visited and inspected the N.E.V. & the animals of the following units of 2nd and 3rd Field Ambulances. The 5th & 157th and 338th Company Divisional Train R.S.C. The new staff Sergeant arrived at Mobile Veterinary Section from No 13 Vet Hospital	
"	14.7.17		Attended Inspection of Officers at H.Q.V.S. VI Corps. Visited and inspected animals of 3rd & 8th Bde R.F.A. Inspected animals in Mobile Veterinary Section	

Original

Army Form C. 2118.

WAR DIARY
or
INTELLIGENCE SUMMARY.
(Erase heading not required.)

F.A.V.C., 62nd Division

Instructions regarding War Diaries and Intelligence Summaries are contained in F. S. Regs., Part II and the Staff Manual respectively. Title pages will be prepared in manuscript.

Place	Date	Hour	Summary of Events and Information	Remarks and references to Appendices
Advanced Remounts	15.7.17		Visited and inspected animals of Divisional Head Quarters. The M.M.P., M.V.S. and the 316th Bde R.F.A.	
"	16.7.17		Visited and inspected the animals of the 248th Bde. R.F.A. with the B.A.C. and transport. Removal seemed too slight. Many of the later gassed to a to eye skin cases and in some animal. Thought not to be suffering. The overcast looks out again. Visited and inspected animals of the S.S. Company Divisional Train and Mobile Veterinary Section	
"	17.7.17		Visited and inspected the animals of the 187th Infantry Brigade. Several animals belonging to the 2/5 Y. & L. Regiment were badly injured on the night of the 16th inst by shell fire. 3 evacuated, 4 shell wounds and 3 died. Inspected animals in 213th Machine Gun Co. and the 3 Sections of 10. 20	
"	18.7.17		Inspected animals in M.V.S. the 185th and 186th Infantry Brigades, the 301st Machine Gun Co. and Divisional Signal Company	
"	19.7.17		Visited the Mobile Veterinary Section. Inspected the animals of the 465th & 468th Company R.E.	
"	20.7.17		Visited and inspected the animals of the 310 Bde R.F.A., 2nd 3rd Brigades R.F.A. & M.V.S.	
"	21.7.17		Attended a conference of A.D.V.S. at the Office of D.D.V.S. 8th Corps. Visited and inspected in M.V.S. the 52nd Company 157th Company & 158th Company Divisional Train	B.V.O.

Original

Army Form C. 2118.

Instructions regarding War Diaries and Intelligence Summaries are contained in F.S. Regs., Part II. and the Staff Manual respectively. Title pages will be prepared in manuscript.

WAR DIARY
or
INTELLIGENCE SUMMARY.
(Erase heading not required.)

D.R.O.V.S.
62nd Division

Place	Date	Hour	Summary of Events and Information	Remarks and references to Appendices
Havincourt Commenced diary	22.7.17		Visited and inspected animals in the following units. The 95th H.L. 208th Machine Gun Company. Horse & Batteries of the 293rd Brigade R.F.A. and the Mobile Veterinary Section	
"	23.7.17		Accompanied the A.D.V.S. 6th Corps during his inspection of the following units. 311th F.R.I. M.D.S. the animals of No 3 Section D.A.C., 466th Company R.E. B & C Batteries 302nd Bde R.F.A. The sick and inspected the animals of No 1 & No 2 Sub sections 1st Brigade	
"	24.7.17		Accompanied the A.D.V.S. 6th Corps on his inspection of the animals of A & D Batteries 3rd H Bde R.F.A. also A, B, C & D Batteries 312th Brigade R.F.A. Visited and inspected the animals in M.V.S. 461st Company R.E. Capt Stewart A.C.6 1.0. 16 310 Bde gone on leave	
"	25.7.17		Visited the Mo V.S. Inspected the animals in No 2 and 3 Section D.A.C. Many of the remount mules sent to join No 3 Section Short outbreak of skin disease. 6 have been isolated as suspects. Range Inspected horses of the M.T. B. D Batteries 293rd Brigade R.F.A. No 13 No 4 Machine Gun Company.	
"	26.7.9		Visited and inspected animals for evacuation 311/6 R) m.V.S. Inspected animals of the 31 Coy 7/3 4 (6 R) Field Ambulance	
"	27.7.17		Visited inspected the animals in 3rd A Bde R.F.A. Visited the Mobile Veterinary Section	
"	28.7.17		Visited inspected the animals in 3, 4 Bde R.F.A. attended Conference at A.D.V.S. 6 Corps	JWG

Original

Army Form C. 2118.

WAR DIARY
or
INTELLIGENCE SUMMARY.
(Erase heading not required.)

Instructions regarding War Diaries and Intelligence Summaries are contained in F. S. Regs., Part II. and the Staff Manual respectively. Title pages will be prepared in manuscript.

Place	Date	Hour	Summary of Events and Information	Remarks and references to Appendices
Avonmouth				
Commanded	29.7.7		Visited and inspected animals of 525 Company No 2 Train and N°3 Section D.A.C.	
"	30.7.7		Inspected animals in the following units 164th Infantry Brigade N°2 Section D.A.C. 208th 21st Machine Gun Company and 44sig Company R.E.	
"	31.7.7		Visited and inspected animals in the following units. The M.V.S. 183rd Infantry Bde 552th Sig & 508 Company Div Train	

P.M^{ill} Major ava
D.A.D.V.S. ?? Div

T7134. Wt. W708—776. 500000. 4/15. Sir J. C. & S.

Original

Confidential
War Diary
of
H.A.F.A.

From 1–8–17 . To 31–8–17

Vol VIII

Vol X 8

Original

Army Form C. 2118.

D.A.D.V.S.
62nd Division

WAR DIARY
or
INTELLIGENCE SUMMARY.
(Erase heading not required.)

Instructions regarding War Diaries and Intelligence Summaries are contained in F. S. Regs., Part II. and the Staff Manual respectively. Title pages will be prepared in manuscript.

Place	Date	Hour	Summary of Events and Information	Remarks and references to Appendices
Permanent Command ship	1.8.17		Visited and inspected animals in 2/1 (W.R.) Mobile Veterinary Section. The Hours 7/3 (W.R.) Field Ambulance & the 185th Infantry Brigade	
	2.8.17		Visited the M.V. Section. Inspected animals in No 1 Section D.A.C. and A.T. Batteries 311th Bde. R.F.A.	
	3.8.17		Accompanied the VI Corps Horse advisor during his inspection of L.D. horse mares in 310 & 311 Bde R.F.A. Inspected animals in 313th Bde R.F.A. Visited the M.V.S.	
	4.8.17		Attended a conference at 1.10 p.m. office VI Corps. Visited and inspected the animals at No 1, 2 & 3 Sections D.A.C. & Mobile Veterinary Section	
	5.8.17		Visited 2/1 (W.R.) M.V.S. Inspected animals in H.Q. R.E. and R.F. the Divisional Signal Co. & Four Company Divisional Train	
	6.8.17		Examined the horse masks recently by remount Officers and horse annexe VI Corps at Divisional H.Q. D.A.C. & R.E. Visited and inspected animals in the 185th & 186th Infantry Bde. Visited Mobile Veterinary Section	
	7.8.17		Visited and inspected the animals in the following units. 2/1 W.R. 2/3 L.R.H. Machine Gun Company 310th Bde R.F.A. 2/1 and 2/3 (W.R.) Field Ambulance and Mobile Veterinary Section	
	8.8.17		Inspected the animals of the 1st Brigade R.F.A. Visited the Mobile Veterinary Section	

Army Form C. 2118.

WAR DIARY
or
INTELLIGENCE SUMMARY.
(Erase heading not required.)

D.T.D.V.S.
65th Division

Instructions regarding War Diaries and Intelligence Summaries are contained in F.S. Regs., Part II. and the Staff Manual respectively. Title pages will be prepared in manuscript.

Place	Date	Hour	Summary of Events and Information	Remarks and references to Appendices
Movement Commenced	9.8.17		Visited and inspected animals in 460 & 461st Companies R.E. & Divisional Signal Company and Mobile Veterinary Section.	
	10.8.17		Visited and inspected animals in No. 1, 2 and 3 Sections D.A.C. There are still traces of Suspected Mange occurring in the last batch of remount reinforcements by No. 3 Section. Forwarded a Conference of D.T.V.S. Report to Office of D.D.V.S. XI Corps	
	11.8.17		Visited and inspected the Mobile Veterinary Section. Suggest in the Divisional eliminating horse show.	
	12.8.17		Accompanied A.D.V.S. XI Corps on his inspection of animals of Nos 4 & 5 Sections D.A.C. and 1/1 & 1/3 Field Ambulance. Inspected animals in 525, 526, 527, 528 Companies Divisional Train	
	13.8.17		Visited 2/2 (W.R.) M.T.S. Inspected animals in 32nd Brigade R.F.A.	
	14.8.17		Visited & inspected the animals in the following units 207, 208, 212, 213 Machine Gun Companies, 185 Company R.E. and 184th R. Stanley Brigade	
	15.8.17		Visited the 65th Division M.V. Section at Beislieux and inspected new apparatus used in treatment of Mange. Inspected the animals of the 185 & 186 Infantry Brigades	

Original

Army Form C. 2118.

WAR DIARY
or
INTELLIGENCE SUMMARY.
(Erase heading not required.)

O.A.D.V.S.
3rd Division

Instructions regarding War Diaries and Intelligence Summaries are contained in F.S. Regs., Part II. and the Staff Manual respectively. Title pages will be prepared in manuscript.

Place	Date	Hour	Summary of Events and Information	Remarks and references to Appendices
Monmouth Commencing	16.8.17		Visited and inspected animals of the 30th Bde R.F.A. The condition of the animals is not near so good as it was 3 weeks. It is hoped inspection for the horses & mules will soon be resumed.	
"	17.8.17		Visited the Mobile Veterinary Section. Visited and inspected animals of the following units. Divisional Signal Company. The 525, 526, 527, 528 Companies, Div & Train	
"	18.8.17		Visited and inspected the animals of the 466, 467 Stn Companies R.E. & 1/1st (103rd) Field Ambulance	
"	19.8.17		Visited and inspected the animals on Nos 1, 2, & 3 Sections D.T.C. and 323 Company Div Train	
"	20.8.17		Visited & inspected the animals on 3rd Bde R.F.A. 160 & 161 & 86th Infantry Brigades	
"	21.8.17		Visited & inspected animals of 41st Bde R.F.A. 201, 212, 2137 & 108 Machine Gun Companies	
"	22.8.17		Visited Mobile Veterinary Section. Inspected animals of the 187 Infantry Bde & Divisional Signal Company.	
"	23.8.17		Inspected animals on the MR1 Mobile Veterinary Section. 330, 331, & 338 Coyes Div Train	
"	24.8.17		Visited Mobile Veterinary Section. Inspected animals on N° 1, 2 & 3 Sections D.T.C.	
"	25.8.17		Inspected animals on 1/1 & 1/3 (103) Field Ambulances. 325 Company Div Train	
"	26.8.17		C & D Batteries 30th Bde R.F.A. also M(oR) M.P.S." The animals on 30 Bde are looking slightly in condition partly due to the neglect of the grazing returning as good.	CSH

Original

Army Form C. 2118.

Instructions regarding War Diaries and Intelligence Summaries are contained in F. S. Regs., Part II. and the Staff Manual respectively. Title pages will be prepared in manuscript.

WAR DIARY
of
INTELLIGENCE SUMMARY.
(Erase heading not required.)

D.A.D.V.S. 62nd Division

Place	Date	Hour	Summary of Events and Information	Remarks and references to Appendices
Monument Commanding	26.8.17		Inspected the animals in the following units. The Hors. & Batteries 310th Bde R.F.A. 185 and 186th Infantry Brigades and 207th Machine Gun Company. Visited Mobile Veterinary Section	
"	27.8.17		Visited and inspected animals in the following units. 7/9 208th 213 213 Machine Gun Company and 2/1y 2nd Field Company R.E. Visited inspected animals for evacuation in Mobile Veterinary Section	
"	28.8.17		Visited and inspected animals in the 311th Bde R.F.A. and 167th Infantry Bde. There is a perceptible falling off in condition of animals due to the severe weather of the past few days.	
"	29.8.17		Visited and inspected the animals in 525th 526th 527th & 528th Companies Divisional Train and Divisional Signal Company. Visited the Mobile Veterinary Section	
"	30.8.17		Inspected the animals of Nos 1, 2 & 3 Sections D.A.C. The 2/1 & 2/3 West R. Field Ambulance Visited the Mobile Veterinary Section	
"	31.8.17		The D.D.V.S. 3rd Army accompanied by A.D.V.S. VI Corps visited inspected 2/1/16 R.F. Mobile Veterinary Section & looked over Premises for Winter Quarters. Inspected animals in 460 & 461 Companys R.E.	

F.F.Neill Major A.V.C.
D.A.D.V.S. 62nd Division

Original

Vol 9

Confidential

War Diary
of
A.H.Q. 62nd Division

From 1=9=13   To 30=9=14

Volume IX.

Army Form C. 2118.

WAR DIARY
of
INTELLIGENCE SUMMARY.
(Erase heading not required.)

D.A.D.V.S. 62nd Division

Instructions regarding War Diaries and Intelligence Summaries are contained in F.S. Regs., Part II. and the Staff Manual respectively. Title pages will be prepared in manuscript.

Place	Date	Hour	Summary of Events and Information	Remarks and references to Appendices
Monchy				
Common only	1.9.17		Attended a conference at A.D.V.S. VI Corps. Visited and inspected the animals of the 7/1650(?) Field Ambulance and 307th Bde R.F.A. An order for a bulk forage ration of hay and oats in lieu of tray has been issued.	
"	2.9.17		Visited the 301st Mobile Veterinary Section. Visited and inspected the animals of the 313th Bde R.F.A. and 1/3 Section D.A.C. Visited the 2/1(?)R.1 Mobile Veterinary Section.	
"	3.9.17		Visited transported the animals in 1/101 and 2 Battalions D.A.C. 189th Infantry Bde 315,316 M.S. Garage. Visited Mobile Veterinary Section. Inspected animals in the four companies Divisional Train.	
"	4.9.17		166th Infantry Bde. 501, 508th Machine Gun Companies and Divisional Signal Company. Visited M.V.R.1 Mobile Veterinary Section. Inspected animals in 88th Infantry Bde.	
"	5.9.17		Visited 310th Brigade R.F.A. Visited Mobile Veterinary Section.	
"	6.9.17		Inspected animals in 310th Brigade R.F.A. Visited Mobile Veterinary Section.	
"	7.9.17		Visited the Wagon lines and inspected animals of the 2/1 and 2/3 Field Ambulances and 1st Company R.E. and 315th Brigade R.F.A. Visited and inspected animals in Mobile Veterinary Section.	
"	8.9.17		Attended Conference at the A.D.V.S. VI Corps. Inspected the animals of No. 1 & 3 Sections D.A.C. Visited Mobile Veterinary Section.	
"	9.9.17		Visited and inspected the animals in the 556, 557, 558 Companies Divisional Train. The Mobile Veterinary Section and 2/3 Field Ambulance.	

Army Form C. 2118.

WAR DIARY
or
INTELLIGENCE SUMMARY.
(Erase heading not required.)

O.A.D.S. 62nd Division

Place	Date	Hour	Summary of Events and Information	Remarks and references to Appendices
Afforment Command HP	10.9.17		Visited and inspected the remnants of 525 (Company) Armoured train. The 31 & 33 Sieges Armoured Universal Signal Company. M.T.M. S.A.A. and Mobile Veterinary Section	
"	11.9.17		Visited inspected and inspected Mobile Veterinary Section for evacuation. Inspected the animals of B.B. R.F.A	
"	12.9.17		Inspected the animals in the following units 185th 186th Infantry Brigades. The 459th 460 & 461st Companies R.E. Visited the M.E.S	
"	13.9.17		Visited and inspected the animals in No 1, 2 and 3 Cluster Co. D.A.C. the No 1, 2 & 3 Machine Gun Companies & Mobile Veterinary Section	
"	14.9.17		Visited the V.S and four Companies Divisional Train inspected their animals	
"	15.9.17		Inspected animals of 62 Infantry Brigade. The 459 Company R.E. & mobile Vet.Y Section. Visited the 9 Battery R.F.A. attached to this Division. Attended a conference of A.D.V.S. Offices Tr.	
	16.9.17		Took over duties of A.D.V.S. from Major Niall O.C. (T.F). Visited 2/1 and 2/3 (E.R) Field Ambulances, also D.H.Q. and Signal Co of 2nd Div	D.R.O
	17.9.17		Visited 2/2 (W.R) Field Ambulance, D.H.Q. and Sergeant Farrier Lane, Inspector horses for evacuation.	D.R.O

Army Form C. 2118.

WAR DIARY
of
INTELLIGENCE SUMMARY.
(Erase heading not required.)

O.A.D.7.S.
62nd Division

Instructions regarding War Diaries and Intelligence Summaries are contained in F. S. Regs., Part II. and the Staff Manual respectively. Title pages will be prepared in manuscript.

Place	Date	Hour	Summary of Events and Information	Remarks and references to Appendices
Renneval	18-9-17		Visited 3 Brigade Coy of 62 Div Train, S.H.Q. and H.Q. R.B. Visited also 2/(UR) Field Ambulance.	2H
Commercial	19-9-17		Visited S.H.Q. and Signals, also Divisional Train 525 Coy and 2/2(UR) Field Ambulance	F.R.D.
"	20-9-17		That V.O's are issued weekly returns. Visited Divisional Train 3 Brigade Coy. L.F.D.	
			and D.M.G., also 2/1 and 2/8 (UR) Field Ambulances	
"	21-9-17		Visited D.H.Q. also 525 Coy Div Train and Signal Coy.	L.A.S.
"	22-9-17		Attended Conference D.A.R.3's at VI Corps Headquarters. Visited D.H.Q.	F.R.S.
"	23-9-17		Visited D.H.Q. and Signals also 526 Coy A.S.C. & H.Q. R.E. and R.A.	S.H.
"	24-9-17		Visited Div Train 2/1 and 2/3 Field Ambulance and D.H.Q. 62 Div Train	Div R.
"	25-9-17		Sick. Influenza.	
"	26-9-17		Visited D.H.Q., Div Train 525 and 526 Coys also 2/ Field Ambulance.	S/R R.E.s
"	27-9-17		Visited Divisional Train D.H.Q. and 2/3 Field Ambulances	G.R.S.
"	28-9-17		Visited 2/3 (UR) Field Ambulance and Signal Coy also S.H.Q	S.C.S.
"	28.9.17		Returned from 10 days leave & Resumed duty	S.R.E.V. & blop & UG (F)
"	29.9.17		Attended a Conference of O.A.O.V.S at VI Corps Head Quarters. Visited and inspected the animals	
			of No.1, 2 and 3 sections O.A.C. also animals of Divisional Signal Company	master O.A.D.V.S. 62nd Div

Army Form C. 2118.

WAR DIARY
or
INTELLIGENCE SUMMARY.
(Erase heading not required.)

O.A.D.15.
62nd Division

Instructions regarding War Diaries and Intelligence Summaries are contained in F. S. Regs., Part II. and the Staff Manual respectively. Title pages will be prepared in manuscript.

Place	Date	Hour	Summary of Events and Information	Remarks and references to Appendices
Movement Commenced	30.9.17		Tested and inspected 2/(W.R.) Mobile Veterinary Section in their Winter Quarters at Tournel. Inspected the animals on the following Units & 310 Brigade R.F.A. The Hants 2/5 (Howz) Field Batteries, The 185 & 186 Infantry Brigades, the 301, 312 & 313 Machine Gun Companies. The condition of the animals in the 1/6, 7, 47 Duke of Wellington is not up to usual standard. The same remark applies to A & B Batteries 310 Bde R.F.A. O'Neill Major A.V.C. D.A.D.V.S., 62nd Division	

Original

Vol 10

Confidential
War Diary
of
D.A.H.Q. 62nd Division
to
From 1-10-17   31-10-17.
Volume X

Original

Army Form C. 2118.

WAR DIARY
or
INTELLIGENCE SUMMARY.
(Erase heading not required.)

A.V.D.S,
63rd Division

Instructions regarding War Diaries and Intelligence Summaries are contained in F.S. Regs., Part II. and the Staff Manual respectively. Title pages will be prepared in manuscript.

Place	Date	Hour	Summary of Events and Information	Remarks and references to Appendices
Armentières	1.10.17		Visited and inspected the animals in the following units of 31st Brigade R.F.A. 187th Infantry Brigade as well as Machine Gun Company. Inspected the animals at the Mobile Veterinary Section for evacuation	
"	2.10.17		Visited Bequires Railhead. Saw arrangements made for entraining etc of animals that were being evacuated. Visited & inspected the animals of the 60th Field Ambulance the 553rd, 556th, 557th & 558th Companies Divisional Train. Under the Mobile Vet. Section	
"	3.10.17		Visited the 2/(60?) Mobile Veterinary Section. Inspected the animals in the following units M.M.G.S. The 460th, 461st & 457th Companies R.E.	
"	4.10.17		Visited and inspected the animals in No 1, 2 and 3 Lectures D.A.C. Had a conference of Veterinary Officers. Visited the Mobile Veterinary Section	
"	5.10.17		Visited and inspected the animals in the following units B. 310th Brigade R.F.A. No 2/3 (60?) Field Ambulance. and 186th Infantry Brigade. Inspected animals at Mobile Gun Company yesterday. That was "Hotchkiss" proven to this depot & are now in 211.	
"	6.10.17		Attended Conference of A.D.V.S at the Offices of A.D.V.S IV Corps. Inspected animals of 186th Infantry Brigade. Visited the Mobile M.V.S	
"	7.10.17		Visited and inspected animals in 31st Bde R.F.A. and Mobile Veterinary Section. B.B. Neill	

Original

Army Form C. 2118.

WAR DIARY
of
INTELLIGENCE SUMMARY. D.A.D.V.S. 62nd Division.
(Erase heading not required.)

Instructions regarding War Diaries and Intelligence Summaries are contained in F.S. Regs., Part II. and the Staff Manual respectively. Title pages will be prepared in manuscript.

Place	Date	Hour	Summary of Events and Information	Remarks and references to Appendices
Havrincourt	8.10.17		Visited the new area around Haplincourt. Noted that we are moving into, also the site for Mobile Veterinary Section at Meand. There are no stables in the area and few standings. Inspected Divisional Head Quarters animals including Signal Company.	
"	9.10.17		Visited 31 (6R) M.V.S. and inspected animals for evacuation. Inspected the animals in 310th Bde R.F.A. Visited D.A.D.V.S. 3rd Division. 163rd Infantry Bde. Visited the M.V.S. Sections of Respective Division.	
"	10.10.17		Visited and inspected the animals of No 1, 2 and 3 Sections D.A.C. Inspected animals of D Battery 310 th Bde R.F.A. and B Battery 311th Bde R.F.A.	
"	11.10.17		Inspected the animals of 525 Company Divisional Train. The M.M. Vans. Divisional Signal Company. Visited the H(GR) Fr.F.S.	
Haplincourt	12.10.17		Moved from Havrincourt. Commanity to new Head Quarters near Haplincourt. The 31 (6R) Mobile Veterinary Section moves to be housed. Inspected animals of Head Quarters.	
"	13.10.17		Attended Conference of D.A.D.V.S. at A.D.V.S. Office to Corps. Inspected the animals of the 165th Infantry Bde. The 2/1st R1 Field Ambulance. The 208 M.V.G. Co. and 516 & 518 Company Division T.	
"	14.10.17		Visited Mobile Vet'y Section. Inspected animals of the 166th Infantry Bde. 460 & 461 Company R.E.	

Original

Army Form C. 2118.

Instructions regarding War Diaries and Intelligence Summaries are contained in F.S. Regs., Part II. and the Staff Manual respectively. Title pages will be prepared in manuscript.

WAR DIARY
of
INTELLIGENCE SUMMARY.
(Erase heading not required.)

D.A.D.V.S. 62nd Division

Place	Date	Hour	Summary of Events and Information	Remarks and references to Appendices
Camp N.W. Haplincourt	14.10.17 *(continued)*		Inspected the animals of the 2/3 Field Ambulance. The 201st Machine Gun Company.	
"	15.10.17		Inspected the animals of the following units in the new area. Hq. 213th M.G.C. 213th (Div) Field Ambulance. The 186th Infantry Bde. The 405th Company R.E. and Divisional Signal Company. Visited and inspected animals of the 310th Brigade R.F.A. 311th Brigade R.F.A.	
"	16.10.17		526th Company A.S.C. and No. 1, 2 & 3 Sections D.A.C. also 457 Company A.S.C.	
"	17.10.17		Visited and inspected the animals of the 185th Infantry Bde. the 405th Company R.E. the 311 M.S.C. Mobile Veterinary Section and 526 & 528th Companies Divisional Train.	
"	18.10.17		Visited and inspected the animals of the following units. The 187th Infantry Bde. 208th Machine Gun Company. 461, 407th Field Company of R.E. and 2/3 Field Ambulance. Visited the 2/1 (62nd) Mobile Veterinary Section.	
"	19.10.17		Inspected the animals in the 186th Infantry Bde. 2/1 (62nd) Field Ambulance & 407 Company R.E. 201 & 233rd Machine Gun Company.	
"	20.10.17		Attended a Conference of D.D. & D.D.V.S. at A.D.V.S. Office IV Corps. Visited and inspected the animals in 2/1 (62nd) Mobile Veterinary Section. 526 and 528th Company Divisional Train.	
"	21.10.17		Visited and inspected the animals in the following units. 2/3, 310th, 311th Brigades R.F.A. No. 1, 2 & 3 Sections D.A.C. and 526 Company Divisional Train.	

B.S.N.

Original

Army Form C. 2118.

D.A.D.V.S.
62nd Division

WAR DIARY
INTELLIGENCE SUMMARY.
(Erase heading not required.)

Instructions regarding War Diaries and Intelligence Summaries are contained in F.S. Regs., Part II. and the Staff Manual respectively. Title pages will be prepared in manuscript.

Place	Date	Hour	Summary of Events and Information	Remarks and references to Appendices
Camp at W Hophurcourt	22.10.17		Accompanied the D.A.Q.M.G. on Inspection of Mobile Veterinary Section at the new premises at Freund. Inspected the animals of 526 and 528 Company Divn Train.	
"	23.10.17		Inspected the animals of the following units at their wagon lines: the 184th Infantry Bde, the 461st Company R.E, 7/3 Field Ambulance, 208th Machine Gun Company, Tests No. 5.	
"	24.10.17		Inspected the Transport horses of the Division at the wagon lines of 526 Company assigned to D.A.Q.M.G. Visited and inspected the animals of the 186th Infantry Bde, 7/(LR) Field Ambulance, the 457th Company R.E, the 201st & 213th Machine Gun Companies.	
"	25.10.17		Inspected animals of Divisional Head Quarters, Head Quarters R.A, H and R.E, the M.M.Q and Divisional Signal Company. Had a Conference of Veterinary Officers.	
"	26.10.17		Visited and inspected the animals of 310th Bde R.F.A, Nos 1, 2 & 3 Sections D.T.C.	
"	27.10.17		525 Company D.T.C and 55y Company D.T.C. Attended Conference at D.D.V.S. Office IV C(?)A(?) Inspected animals in 526 and 528 Companies 17.30	Visits H(L.R) Mobile Veterinary Section
"	28		Visits and inspects animals of 186th Infantry Bde, the 457th Company R.E & 407 Field Ambulance. Had two answers from to meet.	
"	29.10.17		Visited H(L.R) M.V.S. His and horses on the spot to Monchies	

T2134. Wt. W708–776. 500000. 4/15. Sir J. C. & S.

Original

Army Form C. 2118.

Instructions regarding War Diaries and Intelligence Summaries are contained in F. S. Regs., Part II. and the Staff Manual respectively. Title pages will be prepared in manuscript.

WAR DIARY
of
INTELLIGENCE SUMMARY.

O.I. O.I.S. 63rd Division.

(Erase heading not required.)

Place	Date	Hour	Summary of Events and Information	Remarks and references to Appendices
Foreceum	30.10.17		Left Camp near Haplincourt and arrived at Foreceum. No 2/(W.M.) Mobile Veterinary Section moved from Ervillers and remained here during the night of 30th	
"	31.10.17		Remaining Infantry Brigade of the Division left a.m. and arrived in Lorry and bivouaced. The advance of the Division left behind to collect kits and impedimenta the advance of the following Units at Barly 556th Company R.E. two Infantry Battalions 231(W.R.) Field Ambulance, the arrival of the Remaining two Battalions at Barnencourt. The 215th Machine Gun Company at Louerlaire. MG.O.T.C to 75 arrived at Monchiet. 17.25 men from Convalescent Depots. The Stores of Divisional Head Quarters, Signal Company & Divisional W.H.Q.S. M.E.S.	

G.F. Neill Major A.D.C
O.I. O.I.S. 63rd Division

Original

Vol 11.

Confidential

War Diary
of
H.I.H.S. Ward Torr

From 1ˢᵗ/17   To 30ᵗʰ/

Chron 1ˢᵗ/17   Vol: XII

Original

Army Form C. 2118.

WAR DIARY
of
INTELLIGENCE SUMMARY.
(Erase heading not required.)

D.A.D.V.S
62nd Division

Instructions regarding War Diaries and Intelligence Summaries are contained in F. S. Regs., Part II. and the Staff Manual respectively. Title pages will be prepared in manuscript.

Place	Date	Hour	Summary of Events and Information	Remarks and references to Appendices
Toseuse	1.11.17		Visited Group and Inspected the animals of the following Units. 2/5 & 2/4 Duke of Wellington. 457th Company R.E. and 525th Company F.S.C. Inspected at Senescourt the animals of the 2/4 & 2/6 Duke of Wellington. 2/4 K.O.Y.L.I. and 2/5 York and Lancs. Inspected at Beauville animals of the 2/5 K.O.Y.L.I. 2/4 Y&L. 208 Machine Gun Company and 2/3 Field Ambulance & 528th Company Divisional Train.	
"	2.11.17		Inspected the following animals at Toseuse. Div. H.Q. Grs. Div. Signal Company 2/6 West Yorks and M.M.P. At Bady inspected the animals of the 7(GR) Field Ambulance 2/5 West Yorks. Head Quarter 185th Infantry Bde. At Beaumount the 2/4 & 2/5 West Yorks.	
"	3.11.17		Attended Conference at A.O.V.S Officer XVII Corps. Inspected animals of 459 Company R.E and 15/4 Company A.S.C	
"	4.11.17		Visited M.V.S at Movelied. Inspected animals of 2/6 West Yorks. Divisional Signal Company	
"	5.11.17		Inspected animals of 187th Infantry Brigade, 2/3 Field Ambulance. 208th Machine Gun Company. 558th Company Divisional Train. 2/4 & 2/6 Duke of Wellington	
"	6.11.17		Visited and inspected animals in the 185th Infantry Bde. The 2/01 & 2/2 & Machine Gun Company. 2/(SR) Field Ambulance and 2/(6SR) Mobile Veterinary Section	

Original

Army Form C. 2118.

WAR DIARY
or
INTELLIGENCE SUMMARY.
(Erase heading not required.)

T.J. 4-7-15   63rd Division

Instructions regarding War Diaries and Intelligence Summaries are contained in F. S. Regs., Part II. and the Staff Manual respectively. Title pages will be prepared in manuscript.

Place	Date	Hour	Summary of Events and Information	Remarks and references to Appendices
Louvain	7.11.17		Visits and inspects the animals of the 7/6 J.E. Divisional Head Quarters, Divisional Signal Company.	
"	8.11.17		Visits and inspects the 7/(6R) No. 75 at Moorslede. Inspects the animals of the following units at Foury 53rd Company A.S.C. 7/5 and 7/7 Duke of Wellington's	
"	9.11.17		Visits 7/(6R) Mobile Veterinary Section. Inspects the animals of the 186th Infantry Brigade	
"	10.11.17		Inspects the animals of the 7/5 J.E. 74 L.O.T.C.S. 7/(6R) Field Ambulance and 57th Company R.A.S.C	
"	11.11.17		Inspects animals in M.V.S for evacuation. Inspects animals of the 187 Infantry Brigade, 210 & 213 Machine Gun Companies and the 7/3 (6R) Field Ambulance also 558th Company R.A.S.C	
"	12.11.17		Visits 7/(6R) M.V.S. Inspects animals of the 208th Squadron Machine Gun Companies at Melaine.	
"	13.11.17		Still inside in this area on the move to II Corps Area. M.V.S moves to Roslisle, Petit	
Haspres & Wargnies 14.11.17			Move from Louvain to Haplaincourt. The M.V.S moved from Roslisle Petit to Barrastre.	
"	15.11.17		Staff happens to form the 7th Guerden as instructions from II Corps S.R.	

KM

Original

Army Form C. 2118.

WAR DIARY
of
INTELLIGENCE SUMMARY.

A.D.V.S.
62nd Division

(Erase heading not required.)

Instructions regarding War Diaries and Intelligence Summaries are contained in F. S. Regs., Part II. and the Staff Manual respectively. Title pages will be prepared in manuscript.

Place	Date	Hour	Summary of Events and Information	Remarks and references to Appendices
Haplincourt	15.11.17		The M.G.S arrived at Barastre from Rocket Le Petit. Indicated by arrow from II Corps for A.D.V.S. to join the 41st Division on the Bapaume–Cambrai Rd this move was anticipated by 6 p.m. Today A.D.V.S II Corps re-arranged by wire and discussed the investigation of MOR.M.G.S & the Hd qrs are working in temporary quarters during operations. Inspected the veterinary work of the following units. 1/3, 59th Company A.S.C. the 7th & 9th K.O.Y.L.I. M.MGR, Field Ambulance. 310 & Brigades R.F.A. and 311 & Brigades R.F.A. The condition of the animals has not improved since I inspected about 3 months ago. The latter remark applies to Artillery work and particularly to C. Battery 310 Bde, in two divisions to have now made in B. 311 Brigade and A Battery 310 & Brigade. The greater wear now being shown by animals of both brigades is owing to shows prior & a number of Indistinctive animals of the work in retirement will have serious consequences later.	
	16.11.17		Accompanied the DDVS 56 Division & arrange an advance veterinary Collecting Post at Ytres and inspected remounts of the 466 & 461 Companies R.E. Inspected the 310 & 311 Brigades R.F.A. nothing to add to my remarks of yesterday	
	17.11.17		Attended Conference at A.D.V.S Office II Corps, discussed the activities of advance Veterinary Evacuating Stations, the sites selected were at Lechaquerie & Rupelmont	

Original

Army Form C. 2118.

WAR DIARY
or
INTELLIGENCE SUMMARY.   D.A.D.M.S.
63rd Division
(Erase heading not required.)

Instructions regarding War Diaries and Intelligence Summaries are contained in F. S. Regs., Part II. and the Staff Manual respectively. Title pages will be prepared in manuscript.

Place	Date	Hour	Summary of Events and Information	Remarks and references to Appendices
Hyencourt	17.11.17		The Staff went over to convoy of 1 N.C.O. and two men. The personnel for the first named Stations provided by the M.D.S. of the 56 Division and the others by No 63 36th Division. The arrangements at the 36th Divisional Station to be carried out by the Staff of the M.D.S. of the 63rd Division and those at the 56th Divisional Station by the The Staff of the 56th M.D.S. The Artillery units in this Division to draw to the north of a point of 14 days supplies to the amounts of 525 Company Divisional Train who together moved the latter are not up to the usual standard from my opinion some not fit to issue.	
"	18.11.17		Visits and inspects the following animals. The 197th Infantry Bd., 209th Aberdeen Sea Comp 4 H Field Ambulance and No 61st Company R.E.	
Barastre	19.11.17		Present from Hyencourt to Barastre. Visits D.D.M.S 56 Division & made final arrangements to advanced Veterinary Dressing Station. Visits inspects & commends the evacuation at 11 London Section Bapaume Rd. inspects the animals of the 65th O.D.S.	
"	20.11.17		Visits and inspects the animals in following units Viz 160th Infantry Brigade 166 R.1. Field Ambulance 461st Company R.E. 555, 556, 557, 558 Companies of Divisional Train and the 4/2 (R.N) Field Ambulance also 218th Aberdeen Sea Company 1	

T2134. Wt. W708—776. 500000. 4/16. Sir J.C. & S.

Original

Army Form C. 2118.

Instructions regarding War Diaries and Intelligence Summaries are contained in F.S. Regs., Part II. and the Staff Manual respectively. Title pages will be prepared in manuscript.

D.A.D.V.S. 62nd Division

WAR DIARY
or
INTELLIGENCE SUMMARY.
(Erase heading not required.)

Place	Date	Hour	Summary of Events and Information	Remarks and references to Appendices
Bavaichi	21.11.17		Visited advanced Divisional Head Quarters, and inspected animals belonging to there. Inspected the animals of the 164th Infantry Brigade, the 213th Machine Gun Company, Divisional Signal Company. Visited the advanced Veterinary Aid Post. Ichougouish	
"	22.11.17		Visited and inspected the animals in the following units viz:- 186th Infantry Brigade, 2/1(6R) Field Ambulance, 461st Company R.E. and 213th Machine Gun Company.	
"	23.11.17		Inspected the animals of the following units viz:- 185th & 69th Infantry Brigades, the 457th & 460th Companies R.E., 3/1(6R) Field Ambulance & 213th Machine Gun Coy. There is an appreciable falling off in condition of the animals in all units owing to the strenuous work during present operations. An increase in the number of Debility cases is to be expected.	
"	24.11.17		Visited and inspected the animals of No. 1 and 3 Sections D.A.C., the Divisional Signal Company and Divisional Head Quarters. Handed in office of D.A.D.V.S. II Corps.	
"	25.11.17		Visited and inspected the animals of the 62nd Brigade R.F.A. Moved from Baraichi to Neuville.	
Neuville	26.11.17		Visited and inspected 556, 557 and 558 Companies Divisional Train Animals.	

C.S.W.

Army Form C. 2118.

WAR DIARY
or
INTELLIGENCE SUMMARY.
(Erase heading not required.)

D.A.D.O.S
61st Division

Instructions regarding War Diaries and Intelligence Summaries are contained in F. S. Regs., Part II. and the Staff Manual respectively. Title pages will be prepared in manuscript.

Place	Date	Hour	Summary of Events and Information	Remarks and references to Appendices
Meuvilles	27.11.17		Visited and inspected the arrivals of 2nd Bde. Brigade R.F.A. Arms of the arrivals in their Brigade are getting too considered, particularly in C Battery. The harness in the unit due to the hard usage and condition during the advance made the present week.	
	28.11.17		Inspected the arrivals of the 4th & 5/3 (61st) Field Ambulances	
	29.11.17		Inspected the arrivals of the 184th Infantry Brigade, 520, 521 & 557 Companies R.O.F.	
Hoplincourt	30.11.17		Moved from Meuvilles to Hoplincourt	
"			Inspected the arrivals of the 183rd Infantry Bde, the 1/4 & 1/5 Dukes of Wellington	

B.S. Neill Major
D.A.D.O.S
61st Division

Original

Vol 12

Confidential
War Diary
of
D.A.Q. U.S. 63nd Div.

From 1-12-17   To 31-12-17

Vol XII

Original

Army Form C. 2118.

WAR DIARY
OF
INTELLIGENCE-SUMMARY
(Erase heading not required.)

A.D.M.S. 62nd Division

Instructions regarding War Diaries and Intelligence Summaries are contained in F.S. Regs., Part II. and the Staff Manual respectively. Title pages will be prepared in manuscript.

Place	Date	Hour	Summary of Events and Information	Remarks and references to Appendices
Haplincourt	1.12.17		Attended conference at A.D.M.S. Office, IV Corps. Inspected the animals of the 7/168 Field Ambulance. The 656, 657 and 658 Companies Devonport train.	
"	2.12.17		Attended at A.D.M.S. Office. I Corps. no incidents by wire. Visited 7/(168R) M.V.S. on Bapaume Beaumetz Rd. Inspected Divisional Signal Company animals. A. M. Q. and D.H.Q.	
"	3.12.17		Inspected the animals of the following units: 2/3 (WR) Field Ambulance. 201st, 208th Machine Gun Companies and 187th Infantry Brigade. The M.V.S. moves from Bapaume Beaumetz Road to Bapaume.	
Bapaume	4.12.17		Moved from Haplincourt to Bapaume. Rd to Baillencourt.	
"	5.12.17		Inspected the animals of the 186th Infantry Brigade. 201st & 213th Machine Gun Companies	
Villers Chatel	6.12.17		Moved from Bapaume to Villers Chatel. The 7/(168R) An.V.S. moves from Barbenchicourt to Trevin Capello.	
"	7.12.17		Inspected the animals of the 185th Infantry Brigade. 208th Machine Gun Company. Visited the 7/(168R) M.V.S.	
"	8.12.17		Attended at A.D.M.S. Office XIII Corps. Visited the M.T.S. Inspected animals of the 186 Infantry Bde. 55 & 65y Companies R.A.C. 2/1, 2/2, 2/3 (WR) Field Ambulances	

J.J.Neill

Original

Army Form C. 2118.

WAR DIARY
or
INTELLIGENCE SUMMARY.
(Erase heading not required.)

A.D.V.S. 62nd Division

Instructions regarding War Diaries and Intelligence Summaries are contained in F.S. Regs., Part II. and the Staff Manual respectively. Title pages will be prepared in manuscript.

Place	Date	Hour	Summary of Events and Information	Remarks and references to Appendices
Villers Chatel	8.10.19		Inspected animals of the 461 H Company R.E. and 313 K Machine Gun Company	
"	9.10.19		The cases of Lymphatic Mange in 326 Company R.S.C. sent to M.V.S. for evacuation	
"	10.10.19		Visited and inspected animals of the 326 Company R.S.C. 1/1 & 1/2 Field Ambulances Inspected animals of the 185th Infantry Bde. 313 K.M.G. Company. Visited new area	
"			on D. Coys. to select a site for Mobile Veterinary Section. Inspected animals of Divisional Signal Company and on M.T.	
"	11.10.19		Visited Mobile Veterinary Section.	
Labeuvriere	12.10.19		Moved from Villers Chatel to Labeuvriere. Called on A.D.V.S. I Corps	
"	13.10.19		Visited and inspected the animals of the following units, 1/3 186th Infantry Brigade 2/1(A) Field Ambulance, 213th Machine Gun Company, I.C.	
"	14.10.19		Visited and inspected animals of the 187th Infantry Brigade, 208 Machine Gun Company 1/3 (A) Field Ambulance 338 Company R.I.E. 461 Company R.E.	
"			Motor Lorries from Frevin Capelle to Labeuvriere	
"	15.10.19		Attended conference at A.D.V.S. Office I Corps. Visited and inspected animals of 326 Company R.S.C. 165 Infantry Brigade 1/(A) F.G. Ambulance & 208 M.G. Company	
"	16.10.19		Visited and inspected the animals of the 186 Infantry Bde. Sig. Company 95C 457 Company R.E. & 213 M.G. Company	

S.S. Neill

Original

Army Form C. 2118.

WAR DIARY
of
INTELLIGENCE SUMMARY

(Erase heading not required.)

D.A.D.V.S. 63rd Division

Instructions regarding War Diaries and Intelligence Summaries are contained in F. S. Regs., Part II. and the Staff Manual respectively. Title pages will be prepared in manuscript.

Place	Date	Hour	Summary of Events and Information	Remarks and references to Appendices
Rollencourt	17.10.17		Inspected animals of Divisional Head Quarters, Divisional Signal Company, Head Quarters R.E. and R.E. Inspector Tickets notes Veterinary Section	
"	18.10.17		All units of this Division, home from I Corps area and into XIII Corps area. H.Q.R. M.T. horses from Estaminet to Tinques	
Villers Chatel	19.10.17		Divisional Head Quarters moved from Estaminet to Villers Chatel. Very heavy frost on the 16, 17, 18 & 19th makes the roads difficult for horse transport. Inspected animals of Divisional Signals. 258 Company A.S.C. H.Q.P.'s 2dlo Ambulance	
"	20.10.17		and 15" V.A.D. Called on A.D.V.S. XIII Corps - no one in the office	
"	21.10.17		Visited 1/10.7.P., 7.M.S. Inspected H.S.y & 461 Companies R.E.'s horses, mules and mechanical animals of H.Q. West York & 1/6" K.O.Y.L.I.	
"	22.10.17		Inspected Divisional Head Quarters animals. Divisional Signals	
"	23.10.17		Visited 1/10.7 R.M.S. Inspected the animals of the Dvn of Wellington, the 149 Company R.E., H.Q. Sig Company A.S.C., 213th Company Machine Gun.	
"	24.10.17		Inspected the animals of the following units. 1/5 Duke of Wellington, 2/5 West York, 216 Company R.E.G. The 1/6 & 1/7 West York	
"	25.10.17		Inspected the animals of the following units. 258 Company A.S.C. 461 Company R.E., 1/2 W. Riding Ambulance	

R. Kell

Original

WAR DIARY OR INTELLIGENCE SUMMARY

Army Form C. 2118.

D.A.D.V.S. 63rd Division

Instructions regarding War Diaries and Intelligence Summaries are contained in F.S. Regs., Part II. and the Staff Manual respectively. Title pages will be prepared in manuscript.

(Erase heading not required.)

Place	Date	Hour	Summary of Events and Information	Remarks and references to Appendices
Villers Châtel	25.12.17		Inspected the animals of the H/Q Troops of Wellington and the 1/5 K.O.Y.L.I. Found animals of 535 Company A.S.C. showed signs of itching, they proved not to be clipped and were weeping abnormal.	
"	26.12.17		Visited and inspected H/Q 1st Machine Gun Company animals and the animals of H/Q 1st, 2nd, 3rd & 4th and Divisional Head Quarters	
"	27.12.17		Visited and inspected the animals of the following units :- H/Q H/Q Drakes of Wellington H.Q.R.E. 1st Field Ambulance. H.Q.R.A., Mobile Veterinary Section and 157 Company R.E.	
"	28.12.17		Inspected the animals of the following units :- H/Q 557 Company A.S.C., 223 Machine Gun Company, H/Q K.O.Y.L.I.	
"	29.12.17		Inspected the animals of the following units :- H/Q Duke of Wellington H/Q K.O.Y.L.I. H/Q West Yorks, 536 Company A.S.C. Divisional Employment Company.	
"	30.12.17		Inspected the animals of the following units :- H/Q Head Troops H.Q.R.A., 1st Field Ambulance, 460 Company R.E. 413 Field Ambulance, 558 Company A.S.C. H/S H.V.L.	
"	31.12.17		Visited and inspected the animals of the 3rd Brigade R.F.A. on their regaining the Division. The condition of the animals of the Brigade is very satisfactory considering the strenuous time they have had since Nov'r 30 and the fact that the most of the time they have been without Shelter.	

W. Neill
D.A.D.V.S. 63rd Division

T.134. Wt. W708—776. 500000. 4/15. Sir J. C. & S.

Original

Vol 13

Confidential
War Diary
of
H.Q. A.F.A.
62nd (W.R.) Divn

From 1~1~18 To 31~1~18

Vol. XIII

Signal

WAR DIARY
or
INTELLIGENCE SUMMARY.
(Erase heading not required.)

D.A.D.V.S.
62nd Division

Army Form C. 2118.

Place	Date	Hour	Summary of Events and Information	Remarks and references to Appendices
Villers Chatel	1.1.18		Owing to the condition of the roads it is impossible to visit any of the units	GSh
	2.1.18		Visited and inspected the animals of 313 Brigade R.F.A. on their return to the Division. The animals on this Brigade are in by no means looking in good condition considering the hard work and severe weather they have experienced since Oct 20th	
	3.1.18		Inspected the animals of 515 Company A.S.C. all looking well. Visited and inspected the animals of No 1, 2 and 3 Sections D.A.C. and 7/5 Y.L Battery. All the animals in the D.A.C. are looking well and in good condition considering the hard work they have had during the November offensive and since the truce inland States.	GSh
	4.1.18		Visited and inspected the animals of 311 Brigade R.F.A. A few cases of Glanders were noticed, nearly all getting were present cases. Inspected animals of 7 B.S.M. Tps R.E. and E.L.T and Divisional Headquarters.	GSh
	5.1.18		Visited and inspected the animals on the following units 1/1 Sports. M.T.C. 457th Company R.E. 253 Mounted Tour Company, 457 Company R.E. and 2/1 4/9 R.I. Field Ambulance, also 1/1 troop of Wellington	GSh
	6.1.18		Visited and inspected the animals of 46 Coal Yard 4/9 6 Y & 4/8 6 Y, 356 Company A.S.C. The Mobile Veterinary Section	GSh

T2134. Wt. W708-776. 500000. 4/15. Sir J. C. & S.

Original

Army Form C. 2118.

WAR DIARY
or
INTELLIGENCE SUMMARY.
(Erase heading not required.)

D.A.D.V.S.
62nd Division

Instructions regarding War Diaries and Intelligence Summaries are contained in F. S. Regs., Part II. and the Staff Manual respectively. Title pages will be prepared in manuscript.

Place	Date	Hour	Summary of Events and Information	Remarks and references to Appendices
Villers Chatel	7.1.18		Visited and inspected the animals of No. D of M. and 8 Machine Gun Company. Divisional Signal Company.	O.T.R.
	8.1.18		Inspected the animals of No. 36 of Iron Works. 212 A.M.T.C. 461 Company.	P.E.
Victory Camp	9.1.18		Arrived from Villers Chatel to Victory Camp near Arras. 711(W)A M.T.S moved from Avesgnes to Saryes (near Arras). Inspected the animals of the 187th Infantry Bde. Captain Brown A.V.C. returned from leave.	O.T.R.
	10.1.18		Inspected the animals of the following units. 185th & 186th Infantry Brigades, 556, 557 & 558 Companies L.C.C. 460th Company R.E. These notes within the past week or 10 days an increase in the number of animals suffering from inflammation of the eye, probably due to the severe weather. These cases are being isolated by my orders and are to be of the nature of "Contagious Ophthalmia." Held a conference of V.O's of 2/1(W.R.) & 2/2(W.R.) & 2/3(W.R.) Field Ambulances. Inspected 2/1(W.R.) Field Ambulance animals. Also those of No 4 Hty and 301, 2nd Lt. H. Hty. S.C.	O.T.R.
	12.1.18		Inspected the animals of the 3rd A Bde. R.F.A. 53rd Company A.S.C. Ophthalmia is on the increase in D.T. Bde. R.F.A.	O.T.R.
	13.1.18		Visited and inspected the animals of the following units. 63 460 Company R.E. No 4 Hty. 301 Hty. S.C. 2/3(W.R.) Field Ambulance, M.V.S. 556 & 558 Companies A.S.C.	O.T.R.

Army Form C. 2118.

WAR DIARY
or
INTELLIGENCE SUMMARY. D.A.D.V.S.
(Erase heading not required.)

63rd (R.N.) Division

Place	Date	Hour	Summary of Events and Information	Remarks and references to Appendices
Victory Camp	14.1.18		Met the A.D.V.S. XIII Corps at H(W18) M.D.S by appointment and accompanied him during his inspection of that unit. Proceeded to the A.D.S. of the 63rd Divn and inspected the animals of Bn. C. Bde R.F.A. The condition of the animals was satisfactory.	ettc
"	15.1.18		Visited and inspected the animals of 188 & 189 R.E. & Infantry Brigades. Inspected the animals of the D.A.C. all horses in good health and condition. Improvement that the animals in the Column suffer from Contagious Stomatitis, but caused by a condition in the forage area of the XIII Corps seem to be free of F.O.M. Visited and inspected the animals of the following units Hq 4th Bn. 76 K.O.Y.L.I. 1/5 Y&L 308th M.G.C. and Divisional Signal Company	ettc
"	16.1.18		Visited Hd.Qrs A.D.V.S. 2nd Corps, NN Corps. During his inspection of Horselines. Visited and inspected the command of 336, 31, & 7 D Companies M.G.C.	6 etc
"	17.1.18		Met A.D.V.S. XIII Corps by appointment at D.A.C. Wagon lines. Accompanied him during his inspection of the Three sections. Hd. Qrs. Officers of Hd.Qrs Reserve and tractors of 315 Bde R.F.A. 6 etc. B of D. Battery 3rd Bde R.F.A.	ettc
"	18.1.18		Visited and inspected the animals of 329th Bde R.F.A. and in 315 P.Bde. the animals were not visible	Attc

Original

Army Form C. 2118.

WAR DIARY
or
INTELLIGENCE SUMMARY. D.A.T.S.
63rd (N.R.) Division

(Erase heading not required.)

Instructions regarding War Diaries and Intelligence Summaries are contained in F. S. Regs., Part II. and the Staff Manual respectively. Title pages will be prepared in manuscript.

Place	Date	Hour	Summary of Events and Information	Remarks and references to Appendices
Victory Camp	19.1.18		Accompanied C.R.A. 25 x 110 Corps during his inspection of the following units:— 201st Machine Gun Company, 7/1 Field Ambulance, 468 Company F.E. Visits and inspected the animals of 2/1.5 Y.H., 2/15 & 7/15 N.O.S.F., 201st Machine Gun Corps and the Hy, 4/4, 5/4 West York units	88.20
	20.1.18		Visits W.S.R. Mobile Veterinary Section. Inspected the animals of the 4/5 West Yorks.	
	21.1.18		1 Machine Gun Company, 535 Company A.S.C. 36 x 4/5 Divs. of Duke of Wellington 68th Brigade RFA now Bts D Batteries Visits and inspected the animals of 315th Brigade R.F.A. The condition of the stables Picqueting of these Brigades is now unsatisfactory and I cannot but keep the condition will improve. I notice a fallen off suddenly the animals met Battery 310th Bdr and D Battery 311th Bdr are the least satisfactory. The animals of 76 Hy mounted regiment a little have alterations in the management	88. ffm
	22.1.18		Visits + inspects the animals of 314th Brigade R.F.A. and BC + D Batteries 3rd H.Bde — ffm Inspects the animals of the following units:— 1/4 & 1/5 Duke of Wellington, 3/(H.R.) Field Ambulance 5/3 H Company R.E. Details from 56 4th Division M.V.S. and M.M.P	88 Hy.
	23.1.18		Inspects the animals of Q Battery, 3 r K. Bde R.F.A., the D.A.C. M.V.S. Divisional Depot Company	88 Hy

Original

Army Form C. 2118.

WAR DIARY
or
INTELLIGENCE SUMMARY.
(Erase heading not required.)

D.A.D.V.S. 62nd Division

Instructions regarding War Diaries and Intelligence Summaries are contained in F.S. Regs., Part II. and the Staff Manual respectively. Title pages will be prepared in manuscript.

Place	Date	Hour	Summary of Events and Information	Remarks and references to Appendices
Victory Camp	24.1.18		Accompanied the A.D.V.S. XIII Corps during his inspection of 310th Brigade R.F.A.	
"	25.1.18		Held a conference of V.O's of the Division. Attended at Corps during the inspection by D.D.V.S. of animals sent for casting. Inspected the animals of the four Companies Divisional Train. Visited the M.I. Hospital, the Ophthalmia cases there.	
"	26.1.18		Visited and inspected the animals of the 185th, 187th Infantry Bde & the 76 & 79 Bde of Wellington lines, also my Company R.E. Divisional Depot Company, 7208 R.E. Company.	
"	27.1.18		Took over duties of D.A.D.V.S. from Major Hill A.V.C. Inspected 187th Infantry Brigade, and 526 Coy. A.S.C.	
"	28.1.18		Inspected animals of 310th Brigade R.F.A.	
"	29.1.18		Inspected animals of 312th Brigade R.F.A. and 62nd Divisional Train.	
"	30.1.18		Held a Conference of V.O's of the division. Inspected animals of 1/1 PPRE.	
"	31.1.18		and 25th Army Troops R.E.	

J.R. Walts
Capt. AVC
for D.A.D.V.S.

Original

Confidential

Vol 14

War Diary

of

R. A. H. Q.
62nd (WR) Division

From 1-2-18 to 28-2-18

Vol XIV

Original

Army Form C. 2118.

WAR DIARY
or
INTELLIGENCE SUMMARY

(Erase heading not required.)

D.A.D.V.S. 62nd Division

Instructions regarding War Diaries and Intelligence Summaries are contained in F.S. Regs., Part II. and the Staff Manual respectively. Title pages will be prepared in manuscript.

Place	Date	Hour	Summary of Events and Information	Remarks and references to Appendices
Visitors Camp	1-2-18		Inspected animals of 62nd Divisional Train.	
"	2-2-18		Inspected attached units of 56th Division and H.Q. 62 Divn Signals Coy R.E. and H.Q.R.E. and R.A. 62nd Division	DRG
"	3-2-18		Inspected 327 By A.I.B. and 326 By A.I.B.	DRG
"	4-2-18		Conference ADVS XIII Corps and inspected animals of 312 Bde R.I. Bde	
"	5-2-18		Accompanied ADVS XIII Corps and DDVS 1st Army on an inspection of 2/1 (NR) Mobile Veterinary Section.	
"	6-2-18		Inspected animals of 25th Army Corps R.F. and 4/1 Pontoon Park R.E., and Inspected animals of 526 By A.I.E. DRG	
"	7-2-18		Held Conference of Veterinary Officers of the Division. Inspected animals of attached units of 56 Division.	DRG
"	8-2-18		Inspected animals of 525, 526, 527 Bys. 62 Bde Brig. R.F.A.	DRG
"	9-2-18		Inspected animals of 210 Bde R.I.H.	DRG
"	10-2-18		Inspected animals of 525 Coy A.S.C. and attended meeting of Presidents of Horse class held on 25th inst.	DRG
Vellegraff	11-2-18		Office moved to Villa Chatel.	Vellegraff (F)

Army Form C. 2118.

Original

WAR DIARY
or
INTELLIGENCE SUMMARY.
(Erase heading not required.)

Instructions regarding War Diaries and Intelligence Summaries are contained in F.S. Regs., Part II. and the Staff Manual respectively. Title pages will be prepared in manuscript.

O.W.G... 5.F.A.V.S. 5.th (67th) Division

Place	Date	Hour	Summary of Events and Information	Remarks and references to Appendices
Wilton Chalet	12/2/18		Returned from leave and resumed duty. 67FR	
	13/2/18		Visited and inspected the animals of the following units. Viz the HQRS. B.T.O. Hy Hors of Wellington, 213th Machine Gun Company, 55th Company A.S.C., 212th Machine Gun Company, 305th Machine Gun Company, 74 (67th) Field Ambulance, 5/West Yorks, 5/West Yorks. Head Quarters 186th Infantry Brigade, 4th K.O.Y.L.I. and 2/5 (67th) Field Ambulance. 67FR	
"	14.2.18		Inspected the animals in the following units. 3rd Hors. of Wellington M.K.O.Y.L.I., Divisional Signal Company, and the 9th Durham Comfort Brass Bn. 67FR	
"	15.2.18		Visited inspected the animals of the 658th Company A.S.C., 508th Machine Gun Company, 2/16th Field Ambulance, 2/5 York Lancs and Divisional Head Quarters. 67FR	
"	16.2.18		Visited and inspected the animals of the 7th & 9th Hors. of Wellington, 213th Machine Gun Company, 55th Company A.S.C. and 7/(67th) Mobile Veterinary Section. also 55th Company A.S.C. 67FR	
"	17.2.18		Visited and inspected the animals of No 1, 2, & 3 Sections D.A.C., B Battery 307th Bde & Hy Hors.L 67FR	
"	18.2.18		Inspected the animals of B. & D Batteries 307th Bde R.F.A. A Battery 301th Bde R.F.A. and 515 Company A.S.C. also animals for evacuation in Mobile Veterinary Section 67FR	

Army Form C. 2118.

WAR DIARY
INTELLIGENCE SUMMARY.
(Erase heading not required.)

K.F.O.Y.L.I. 69th (2nd) Division

Place	Date	Hour	Summary of Events and Information	Remarks and references to Appendices
Villers Chatel	19.2.19		Visited and inspected the animals of the following units. A & C Batteries 310th Brigade R.F.A. C Battery 311th Brigade R.F.A. 9th Durham Horses Batt. & Divisional Signal Company 69D.	
"	20.2.19		Inspected the animals of the following units at Savoit. 5th K.O.Y.L.I. Band & D Battalion 311th Brigade R.F.A. At Hermin ½ Field Ambulance 208th Machine Gun Company ½ York Lane. At Tranvillers 578 Company A.S.C. At Bethonsart ¾ Duke of Wellingtons Rgt. Had a Conference of N.C.O.'s Veterinary Range & steps to be taken to prevent outbreak of disease. Visited & inspected the animals of the 9th Durham Pioneers also a horse	
"	20.2.19		and 13th Durham sent to the road from 58 & ? Gol Grainers	
"	23.2.19		Visited the M.O.R.S. A.V.S. Inspected the animals of B & D Batteries 311th Bde R.F.A. A Battery 310th Bde R.F.A & 535 Company A.S.C.	
"	25.2.19		Attended a Conference at XIII Corps, discussed Glanders notes names of cases most freqly infomed in the Horses Transports Tracks transports the animals of A & C Battalion 310th Bde R.F.A. — C Battery 311th Bde R.F.A. 13 & D Battalion	
"	26.2.19		Inspected the animals of the following units V3 N° 1, + 73 Larkum D.A.C. 13 & D Battalion 311th Brigade R.F.A and the 5 K.O.Y.L.I. The animals on the 13 & D Battery 311th Brigade R.F.A. on the whole are not in as good condition, as they were a month ago.	

Army Form C. 2118.

Original

Instructions regarding War Diaries and Intelligence Summaries are contained in F.S. Regs., Part II. and the Staff Manual respectively. Title pages will be prepared in manuscript.

WAR DIARY
or
INTELLIGENCE SUMMARY.
(Erase heading not required.)

D.A.D.V.S. 62 (2nd) Division

Place	Date	Hour	Summary of Events and Information	Remarks and references to Appendices
Villers Chatel	24.3.18 Continued		I am of the opinion that the animals of Bar D Battries 313th Brigade R.F.A. stood to be in good in any other Battery in the Division & a little more attention was given to Stablemanagement.	
"	25.3.18		Visited and inspected the animals of the following units: The 2/1 (W.R.) Mobile Veterinary Section. 8/y Vans of Wellingtons. 356 and 507 Companies A.S.C., No.1 st. 2/2. 2/3 Ambulance Companies. 4/5 Field Ambulance. Head Quarters 186th Infantry Bde., 2/6 2/6 & 2/7 West Yorks.	65/16
"	26.3.18		4/5 York & Lancs and 2/3 Field Ambulance. Inspected the animals of the 9th Durham Light Infantry Battalion. 62 (2nd) Divisional Signal Company & M.M.P. Attended Divisional Horse Show.	65/16
"	27.3.18		Visited and inspected the animals of the following units: 1/3 S.H.F.H.L.! (T.F.R.) 4/5 Field Ambulance, 209th Machine Gun Company, 1/5 York and Lancs, 518th Company A.S.C. and the Duke of Wellingtons.	65/16
"	28.3.18		Visited and inspected the animals of A & C Batteries 310th Bde R.F.A. & D Battery 3rd Bde R.F.A.	

J.S. Nield Major AVC
D.A.D.V.S. 62 (2nd) Division

Original

VC 15

Confidential
War Diary
of
A.D.V.S.
62nd (2/W.R.) Division

From 1-3-18   To 31-3-18

Vol: XV

Army Form C. 2118.

WAR DIARY
of
INTELLIGENCE SUMMARY.
(Erase heading not required.)

Original

Instructions regarding War Diaries and Intelligence Summaries are contained in F. S. Regs., Part II. and the Staff Manual respectively. Title pages will be prepared in manuscript.

G.O.O.T.S. 63rd (R.N.) Division

Place	Date	Hour	Summary of Events and Information	Remarks and references to Appendices
Villers Chatel	1.3.18		Visits and inspects the arrival of the following units: V/3 "A" Battery 31st Brigade. Band 3rd Scott Brigade. T.M.(R.F.) Am./T.S.	G.S.M.
"	2.3.18		Visits and inspects the arrival of the 525th Company A.S.C. Divisional Supply Company. 2/HQR Am/T.S. B & D Batteries 13/s R Brigade R.F.A.	G.S.M.
"	3.3.18		Inspects the arrival of 63rd Division D.A.C. Visits 148/501 M.T. & takes a lesson of his journey in accordance with instructions contained in S.R.O. 3470.	G.S.M.
Roclincourt	4.3.18		Moves from Villers Chatel to Roclincourt. Via 3/(R.N.) Am.T.S. moves from Roclincourt to a position E.H. on the Arras Cambrai Road (Aux. 63.s.8). Inspects the arrival of 3/(R.N.) Field Ambulance.	G.S.M.
"	5.3.18		Visits and inspects the arrival of the following Brig. H.Q. 201. 10 P. D.R. & 13. Machine Gun Companies. 457 & 460 M.L. Companies R.E. & 163rd Infantry Brigade.	G.S.M.
"	6.3.18		Inspects the arrival of the journey units. M.G. Sections Machine Gun Company. 536, 537 & 538 Companies No. 3 Section of Reserve Park. 188th Infantry Brigade.	G.S.M.
"	"		G.O.C. visits the A.V.S. also XIII Corps Supp. & Fuel on the Grenadier of this Section. Visits and inspects the arrivals on the following units: 459, 460, 461 Companies R.E. & the 188th Infantry	G.S.M.
"	7.3.18		Brigade Post of M.G.C.	G.S.M.

Army Form C. 2118.

WAR DIARY
or
INTELLIGENCE SUMMARY.
(Erase heading not required.)

D.A.D.V.S. 62nd (2/6R) Division

Place	Date	Hour	Summary of Events and Information	Remarks and references to Appendices
Roisel	8.3.18		Accompanied the A.D.V.S. XIII Corps during the inspection of 312th Brigade R.F.A. and A Battery 312th Brigade R.F.A. Visited 2/1(6R) MVS.	
"	9.3.18		Visited and inspected the animals of the following Units viz; 311th & 312th Machine Gun Companies, the Bn.H.Q. 2/5 York & Lancs., A Battery 312th Bde R.F.A., D Battery 312th Bde R.F.A. and 556 Company A.S.C. The animals of D Battery 312th Bde R.F.A. have gone off in condition for the past month. This is due in my opinion to lack of interest in Stablemanagement and failing to not having sufficient manual at the troops line to look after the animals properly. Visited the 2/1(6R) Mobile Veterinary Section and XIII Corps Hqrs.	
"	10.3.18		Visited & inspected the animals of 1st, 2nd & 3rd Section D.A.C. D Battery 311th Bde R.F.A. Divisional Signal Company, Hut Guards R.A. & Mobile Veterinary Section.	
"	11.3.18		Accompanied the A.D.V.S. XIII Corps during his inspection of the animals of B, C & D Batteries 311th Brigade R.F.A. These are still a good few thin animals in D Battery. Inspected the animals of 2/1(6R) Field Ambulance. Still much sickness. Visited the 24 (6R) MVS.	
"	12.3.18		The 62nd Divisional Signal Company. Inspection of Reserve Park and 4 Forestry Company. Visited & inspected animals of B, C & D Bateries 311th Bde R.F.A. Staff Capt. R.A. present during inspection of B.C.D. Inspected the animals of 208 & 213 M.G.C. & 187th Infantry Brigade.	

Original

Army Form C. 2118.

WAR DIARY
of
INTELLIGENCE SUMMARY.
(Erase heading not required.)

A.D.V.S. 62nd (2/WR) Division

Instructions regarding War Diaries and Intelligence Summaries are contained in F. S. Regs., Part II. and the Staff Manual respectively. Title pages will be prepared in manuscript.

Place	Date	Hour	Summary of Events and Information	Remarks and references to Appendices
Richincourt	13.3.18		Visited and inspected the animals of the following units Viz 457th, 460th, 461st Company R.E. 62nd Divisional Signal Company, C Company, Div. M.G.C. and 31 (W.R.) Mobile Veterinary Section	G.S.R.
"	14.3.18		Visited & inspected the animals of 311th Brigade R.F.A. There is an improvement in the general management of this Brigade. Grooming is better, but requires more attention still. Attended a Conference at the office of the D.D.V.S. XIII Corps and discussed the reclamation of Mobile Veterinary Section Schedule evacuation equipment	G.S.R.
"	15.3.18		Visited and inspected the animals of the 7/3 (W.R.) Field Ambulance. 310th Brigade R.F.A. 255th, 526th, 537th & 538th Company A.S.C. Visited 31 (W.R.) M.V.S.	G.S.R.
"	16.3.18		Visited and inspected the animals of 312th Brigade R.F.A. The grooming and general care of the animals in this Brigade is better, but is not satisfactory yet. It is hoped by constant inspection that the condition of affairs will be remedied. Inspected the animals of the 185th & 166th Infantry Brigade Cars D Companies Machine Gun Battalion	G.S.R.
"	17.3.18		Inspected the animals of No 1, 2 and 3 Sections D.O.C. and A Company of the Divisional Machine Gun Battalion	G.S.R.
"	18.3.18		Attended an inspection by D.D.V.S. 1st Army of the animals of 7th West Essex 7th Divi of Leicesters & 75th M.L. Visited 31(W.R.) M.V.S.	G.S.R.
			Visited and inspected the animals of 311th Brigade R.F.A.	

Army Form C. 2118.

WAR DIARY
or
INTELLIGENCE SUMMARY.
(Erase heading not required.)

D.A.D.V.S. 62nd (2nd) Division

Instructions regarding War Diaries and Intelligence Summaries are contained in F. S. Regs., Part II. and the Staff Manual respectively. Title pages will be prepared in manuscript.

Place	Date	Hour	Summary of Events and Information	Remarks and references to Appendices
Radiscourt	19.3.18		It was reported to me by Telephone message from a D.A.D.V.S. XIII Corps that a mule belonging to the 76 Dn/h Regiment's evacuated by the 31 (62nd) M.V.S. for Ulcerative Colletitis had been diagnosed at the Base Veterinary Hospital as Epizootic Lymphangitis. I visited the horse lines of this unit & day made a careful inspection of every animal and suspicious into the history of the mule in question. It appeared that he contracted the disease had been with the 76 Dn/h to up to 29/1/18 and on re-organisation of the Standing Brigades was handed over to the 76 Dn/h. There was an old standing wound on the outside of the off hetarsal bone extending from half way down the bone to the fetlock. The history of this case has been elicited from information told the latter (E.C.) as an exudate. Four animals in the 76 Dn/h have been treated lately by the last named. Suspected animals of S.S.N. Company R.F.C. visited the mobile Veterinary Section.	
"	20.3.18		Accompanied the D.D.V.S. 1st Army & G.D.V.S. XIII Corps during their inspection of the animals of the 185th Infantry Brigade also the 95 + 76 Dn/h. Inspected the 3rd ? Brigade R.F.A.	65R 65R
"	21.3.18		Inspected the animals of the 76 + 95 Dn/h particularly animals suspected for Epizootic Lymphangitis.	65R

Army Form C. 2118.

WAR DIARY
of
INTELLIGENCE SUMMARY.
(Erase heading not required.)

D.A.D.V.S. 62(?)R. Division

Instructions regarding War Diaries and Intelligence Summaries are contained in F.S. Regs., Part II. and the Staff Manual respectively. Title pages will be prepared in manuscript.

Place	Date	Hour	Summary of Events and Information	Remarks and references to Appendices
Rocquigny	Contd 21.3.18		Visited and inspected the animals on the following units: 3rd & 4th Divl. of Wellingtons By D Battn. 311th Brigade R.F.A. Visited 4/6 R1 M.V.S.	TGR
"	22.3.18		Visited inspected animals of 463 & 464 Coys: supervising the horses in exhibit. The work of disinfecting the stables of these units in progress. Suspected 4% of the floor of B. 29 M. has been removed to the depth of 6 inches to remove noxious being buried in lime. Inspected the animals of 461 Company R.E. Attending a conference at No. V.S. 1st Army and was absent on the work of the veterinary services by the D.V.S. Off.	TGR
"	23.3.18		Accompanied D.D.V.S. XII Corps during the inspection of the 9th Yeos. Amn. 523rd Company A.S.C. Arrived. Visited the 4/6 R1 M.V.S.	TGR
"	24.3.18		Moved from Rocquigny to Warlus 4/6 R1 M.V.S. move from Louis to Beauvelle Lequin at A.D.V.S. office XVII Corps. Inspected animals of Divnl. Signal Coys 7th Field Ambulance G.H. Divnal indicated wishes to "Re inspection parade.	TGR
Warlus	25.3.18			
"	26.3.18		Visited the following places with the object of finding units of the Division. Berles - au - Bois, Bienvillers Simeoncourt. Was unable to find any units except 3 Field Ambulance. Orig & signatures and civilian changing of road was unable to locate any other unit on this date.	TGR
"	27.3.18		Visited the following units at Sombrin 455, 460, 461 Companies R.E. & 9th Durham Light Infantry Battalion	

Army Form C. 2118.

WAR DIARY
of
INTELLIGENCE SUMMARY.
(Erase heading not required.)

D.A.D.V.S 63rd Division

Instructions regarding War Diaries and Intelligence Summaries are contained in F.S. Regs, Part II. and the Staff Manual respectively. Title pages will be prepared in manuscript.

Place	Date	Hour	Summary of Events and Information	Remarks and references to Appendices
Marlies	27.3.18		Visited the animals of 104th Infantry Brigade near Sommes, no casualties reports up to date in this Brigade. Visited the 188th & 189th Infantry Brigade's horse Hammercoy's. One casualty reported in 188th Brigade. Horses now in 189th Brigade. Visits 526 & 534 Companies A.S.C. at Beauvilliers. no casualties. Visits the 63rd Divisional Baseline Gun Battalion. 9 death reports in this Battalion. 9 is animal transport. OFF.B	
"	28.3.18		Visits D/(KA) Mobile Veterinary Section made arrangements as to Evacuation. Attended at Office to receive reports of E.O's as to casualties & to Through Horses relieve OFF.B	
"	29.3.18		Visits G.D.V.S XIII Corps and Transport A.J. Association. Standing by to prepare to move to another area OFF.B	
"	30.3.18		Visits the 63rd Divisional Signal Company & D.A.C at Toncaille. The M(OR) Mobile Veterinary Section. horses from Bonneville to Naours	
"	31.3.18		Standing by ready to move	

F.F.Neill Major a.v.C
D.A.D.V.S 63rd(R.N) Division

August 14

No 16

Confidential
War Diary
of
A.A. & Q.M.G. 62nd (W.R.) Division
Vol. XVI

From 1/4/18   To 30/5/18

Army Form C. 2118.

WAR DIARY
INTELLIGENCE SUMMARY.

D.A.D.V.S. Egypt(N.R.) Division

(Erase heading not required.)

Instructions regarding War Diaries and Intelligence Summaries are contained in F.S. Regs., Part II. and the Staff Manual respectively. Title pages will be prepared in manuscript.

Place	Date	Hour	Summary of Events and Information	Remarks and references to Appendices
Marlus	1.4.18		Visits and inspects the animals of 301st Bde R.F.A. at Beersheba. also D Battery 301st Brigade. The Artillery animals on the whole are standing the Strain of present operations fairly well. The condition of the few the animals in 2nd D Battery 301 Bde has not improved. Inspects the animals of 187 Bde Horse Quarko Coy. Arrives from Hebron to Pao.	
Pao	2.4.18		Visits the 31(6?R) M.F.S. at Hereen. Calls on A.D.M.S. N Corps and inspects stad arrives in this area	
"	3.4.18		Visits and inspects the animals of 65 no Divisional tractive Gun Battalion at Pao. (?) Companies animals seem to have suffered most in recent operations and their condition is not quite so good as they were. Inspects the animals of 53 S and 52 Y d Companies R.S.C. The 31(6?R) M.V.S. moves from Hereon to Pao.	
"	4.4.18		Inspects the animals of the ⅞ Duke of Wellington Visits and inspects the animals of the following units at Hereon. 2/3(6?) Field Ambulance 76 + 3/9 West Yorks. The animals of the last two named units are looking fairly fit considering the hard work and antumn weather. Some animals in the Field Ambulance have lost condition but with better weather conditions should soon pick up again. Inspects at Vavaletta the 9th Durham Loman Battalion animal also those of the 7/9 West Yorks. Visits 3/(6R) D.S.	

WAR DIARY
or
INTELLIGENCE SUMMARY.

Army Form C. 2118.

(Erase heading not required.)

Original

Instructions regarding War Diaries and Intelligence Summaries are contained in F.S. Regs., Part II. and the Staff Manual respectively. Title pages will be prepared in manuscript.

D.A.D.V.S. 62nd Division.

Place	Date	Hour	Summary of Events and Information	Remarks and references to Appendices
Gaza	5.4.18		Visited and inspected the animals of the following units at Amleh. H.Q.Y.L.S. 3/4 Y.E. 461st Company H.T. 326 and 558th Companies A.S.C. 2/4 and 7/5 A.S.C.	
"	6.4.18		All the animals in above units are looking extrapordinary. Visited H(66)R M.V.S. and inspected at Hain the animals of H(66)R Field Ambulance, they're not looking in as good condition as they were a month ago. Visited the new Y.E. Base of Wellington's own 525 Company A.S.C. The animals in this Co. are not in as fit as they should be no doubt the loss of condition is due to increase of work under trying conditions. Inspected the animals of 62nd D.A.C. at Erun. All are looking very fit. Horses from Sea to Hinn. H(66)R) Mobile Veterinary Section moves from Junction to Somake.	
Lefarni afternoon	7.4.18		Visited the units at Somake. Visited 525 Company A.S.C. at Hinn. Visited the H(66)R M.V.S. at Somake. The ride on which this unit was located was as bad arrangements were made to move to the farm Janet the Graham Somake. The move was carried out in the afternoon of this date. Visited the horse lines of 525 & 557th Companies A.S.C. in Somake also the 187th Infantry Brigade Horse lines activities.	
"	8.4.18		The condition of the horses on the night of the road near Somake leaving from Hinn to the Goat Pan Camp, is there in have no two many to condition many unwilling we have had the great plus change & there is little hope of freshness. The animals expend forever on account of the congestion are not here. The animals in totally all work are suffering in condition on consequences of the Red Meather of the Pashotil.	

Army Form C. 2118.

Original

WAR DIARY
of
INTELLIGENCE SUMMARY.   D.A.D.V.S. 63rd Division

(Erase heading not required.)

Instructions regarding War Diaries and Intelligence Summaries are contained in F. S. Regs., Part II. and the Staff Manual respectively. Title pages will be prepared in manuscript.

Place	Date	Hour	Summary of Events and Information	Remarks and references to Appendices
Hamun	9.4.18		Visited the horse lines of 317th Brigade R.F.A. situated on the left of the road at Bienvillers leading to Hannescamps. The animals in this Brigade are still kept in crowded particularly C & D Batteries. It would appear to me that the low condition of many of the animals in these two Batteries is not wholly accounted for by the weather & standings, but more likely to want of interest, care or stable management. (Report sent to Head Quarters on this matter today.) Visited 310th Brigade Wagon Lines on the right of the road between Bienvillers and Souastre. The condition of the animals in this Brigade are satisfactory. 88th Visited the horse lines of the following units at Hamon 41, 42, & 43 Field Ambulances. Vaccine and inspected the animals of the following units Last Infantry Brigade Head Quarters 457, 460 & 461 Companies R.E. and 253rd Infantry Brigade 460 Company R.E. have lost their but wind Shelter will soon put up the animals suffering from windsore the animals of the 8th R.F.S. These are practically all new cases of windsore affection with the Gas. Both are badly affected in the eyes & are in places & Windsore particularly in places where there is little or no hair such as the Udder etc. 88th	
"	11.4.18		Visited and inspected the animals of 1867 Infantry Brigade and the 9th Durham Pioneer Battalion. The Durhams & 4/5 Duke of Wellington's are quite as fit as they should be. 88th	

A5834 Wt. W4973 M687. 750,000 8/16 -D. D. & L. Ltd. Forms/C.2118/13.

Original

Army Form C. 2118.

WAR DIARY
of
INTELLIGENCE SUMMARY.
(Erase heading not required.)

D.J.D.V.S.
62nd (2R) Division

Instructions regarding War Diaries and Intelligence Summaries are contained in F. S. Regs., Part II. and the Staff Manual respectively. Title pages will be prepared in manuscript.

Place	Date	Hour	Summary of Events and Information	Remarks and references to Appendices
Offoux	12.4.18		Visited and inspected the animals of 312th Brigade R.F.A. The horse lines attacked on the night of the 11th had many broken leads and wounders. The standings are great improvement on those of Brunelles and with the continuance of good weather and a little extra attention the poor animals of this Brigade should begin to pick up. Visited and inspected the animals of A.B.& D Companies of the 2nd Div. Train. A few sore backs in B Company are notice than otherwise the pack-away animals are looking satisfactory. Inspected the animals of 526, 527 & 528 Companies A.S.C.	88A
"	13.4.18		Attended a conference at A.D.V.S. Office IV Corps. Inspected the animals of 61st Inf. A.C. at Corun. all are looking fit and in good condition. Visited the 31(401st) Mobile Veterinary Section. The number of evacuations by this Section during the week has been more than usual owing to the first rest has been excavating for Corps troops and these Divisions as well as our own.	87A
"	14.4.18		Visited and inspected the animals of the 71, 7/6 & 7/3 Field Ambulances also 525 Company A.S.C. v Veterinary Mobile Section and 187th Infantry Brigade.	55A
"	15.4.18		Visited and inspected the animals of the following units: 185th, 186th Infantry Brigades, & 460 & 461 Companies R.E. and 310th Brigade R.F.A. also visited respected the animals of 310th & 311th Brigades at rest. Horse lines. Conor. Visited 71/402 M.V.S.	88A
"	16.4.18		Visited inspected the animals at advanced Wagon lines of 311 Bde R.F.A.	

Original

Army Form C. 2118.

WAR DIARY
or
INTELLIGENCE SUMMARY.   C.A.D.V.S.
(Erase heading not required.)   62nd Division

Instructions regarding War Diaries and Intelligence Summaries are contained in F. S. Regs., Part II. and the Staff Manual respectively. Title pages will be prepared in manuscript.

Place	Date	Hour	Summary of Events and Information	Remarks and references to Appendices
Hem	16.4.18		Inspected the animals of 62nd Divisional Machine Gun Battalion. Visited 2/1st M.V.S.	62A
Jan	17.4.18		Horses from them also 3/1st M.Mobile Veterinary Section to San. Inspected the animals of the following units 457, 460 & 461st Companies R.E. and 523rd Company R.E.	62A
"	18.4.18		Visited and inspected the animals of the following units 352nd, 358, 459 & 578 Company R.E. Divisional Signal Company, & 3/1st Mobile Veterinary Section, 185th & 187th Infantry Brigades.	62A
"	19.4.18		Inspected at the Advanced Wagon Lines the animals of 30th Brigade R.F.A. Visited transports & the animals of 186th Infantry Brigade. Inspected animals for evacuation at M.V.S.	62A
"	20.4.18		Attended a conference at A.D.V.S. Office IV Corps. Inspected at the near Wagon Lines the animals of 310th & 311th Brigades R.F.A. Visited inspected animals of the 4th (DR) Field Ambulance. Visited 3/1st M.V.S.	62A
"	21.4.18		Visited and inspected the animals of the 190th Infantry Brigade and R.V.C. Sections of 62nd D.A.C. At Hem Vecl Quentin Drouvin R.A.F. B.A. 93 75 Field Ambulance & Divisional Signal Company. Visited Mobile Veterinary Section.	62A
"	22.4.18		Visited and inspected at the advance wagon lines the animals of 312th Brigade R.F.A. The animals of D Battery are far from satisfactory and unless more interest is taken in them being told to mount be evacuated for debility. There is a slight improvement in the animals of the other Batteries.	58A

Army Form C. 2118.

Original

WAR DIARY
or
INTELLIGENCE SUMMARY.
(Erase heading not required.)

D.A.D.V.S. 62nd Division

Instructions regarding War Diaries and Intelligence Summaries are contained in F.S. Regs., Part II. and the Staff Manual respectively. Title pages will be prepared in manuscript.

Place	Date	Hour	Summary of Events and Information	Remarks and references to Appendices
Fins	22.4.18		Visited & inspected at Sorcastie the animals of A. & B. Companies machine Gun Battalion. Inspected at Sus animals of the 526th, 55th, & 538th Companies A.S.C. also 2/1 (62nd) Field Ambulance. Visited 7(W.R.) M.G.S.	OK
"	23.4.18		Inspected at Henencourt the animals of 2/03 Station D.A.C. 313(W.R.) Field Ambulance. Visited the Horse lines of 9th Durham Pioneers, was unable to see many of the animals as they were out at work. Those that were in are not up to good condition and they lost a month ago & this is hardly attributable to constant hard work, or bad weather. Visited the Mobile Veterinary Section.	OK
Hertbis	24.4.18		Moved from Sus to Hertbis. Visiting the advance wagon lines of 310th Brigade R.H.A. All the animals also at these lines with the exception of Q Battery are keeping fit and in fair condition. Demands have slightly fallen off in Q Battery from effects than I sent to evacuate last week. Visited the Rear Wagon lines of 310th Bde & St. H. at Couen. Animals at D310 & Bde H.Q. suffer from cases of obstinate engagement to the Evening. Evening too in B Battery. Visited & inspected the animals of 184th Infantry Brigade & 460th Company R.E. All their animals are looking very fit.	OK

Army Form C. 2118.

WAR DIARY
INTELLIGENCE SUMMARY.
(Erase heading not required.)

Instructions regarding War Diaries and Intelligence Summaries are contained in F. S. Regs., Part II. and the Staff Manual respectively. Title pages will be prepared in manuscript.

Original

D.A.D.V.S. 63(RN) Division

Place	Date	Hour	Summary of Events and Information	Remarks and references to Appendices
Arcilli	25.11.18		Visited and inspected the animals of the following units. 1/3 Machine Gun Battalion, 188th Infantry Brigade, 2/2 Field Ambulance, 2/3 Field Ambulance, and 157 Company R.E.	8th
"	26.11.18		Inspected the animals of Divisional Head Quarters 188th Infantry Brigade & 256 Company A.S.C. Visited the 31(68th) M.V.S at Sens and inspected an animal sent in by 157 Brigade with digestive troubles. This case is rather suspicious of Epigotic Lymphangitis. Smear was taken and forwarded to No. Veterinary Hospital Rouen for microscopical examination. In the meantime the animal is isolated at the M.V.S pending confirmation or otherwise of Diagnosis. The A.D.V.S. VI Corps visited 31(68th) M.V.S	8th
"	27.11.18		Attended a Conference at A.D.V.S. Office VI Corps. Visited and inspected the animals at 31(68th) M.V.S for evacuation. Had an interview with C.R.A and discussed the condition of the animals of 31st Brigade R.F.A. Errors in stable management and found faults and suggestions made to remedy same.	8th
"	28.11.18		Visited inspected the animals of 310th & 317th Brigades R.F.A. The horses are looking fit. D Battery animals have dropped condition but will soon pick up again. There is an improvement in the animals of 317 R Brigade but D Battery & C Battery & D Battery & far from satisfactory yet. Inspected the animals of 7th Durham Pioneer Battalion	8th

Army Form C. 2118.

WAR DIARY
or
INTELLIGENCE SUMMARY.
(Erase heading not required.)

D.A.D.V.S. 62nd (2nd R) Division

Place	Date	Hour	Summary of Events and Information	Remarks and references to Appendices
Authie	29.4.18		Visited and inspected at Louvencourt 53 remounts this strength is better than those we have had for several months. Inspected all the animals that are in the horse lines of 185th Infantry Brigade. Inspected all the animals of 466th Company R.E., 556th Company L.S.C.	58%
"	30.4.18		Visited & inspected the animals of Divisional Signal Company. N°3 Section D.A.C. 184 Infantry Brigade & 466th Company R.E. The condition of all animals in these units is satisfactory. Visited prospects animals for evacuation at the M/(O.R.) & F.A. at Pas. Inspected animals of 557, 558 L.S.C. at Pas.	58%

B. H. Neill. Major A.V.O.
D.A.D.V.S. 62nd (2nd R) Division

Confidential

Original

War Diary

of

D.A.D.V.S. 63rd (W.R.) Divn

From 1-5-18 To 31-5-18

Vol XVII

Vol 17

Original

Army Form C. 2118.

WAR DIARY
or
INTELLIGENCE SUMMARY.
(Erase heading not required.)

Instructions regarding War Diaries and Intelligence Summaries are contained in F. S. Regs., Part II. and the Staff Manual respectively. Title pages will be prepared in manuscript.

04.0.15 62nd (2W.R) Division

Place	Date	Hour	Summary of Events and Information	Remarks and references to Appendices
Arthies	1.5.18		Visited and inspected the animals of 310th & 311th Brigades R.F.A. 535 Company A.S.C. There is an improvement in the animals of Sir W. Bde. R.F.A. Visits Inspection annual for vaccination ThoR) M.I.5	8TN
"	2.5.18		Inspected the animals of the following units: 186th Infantry Brigade, 1134 Company R.E. and Divisional Machine Gun Battalion. The animals in the 7th Bde of Wellingtons are not in as good conditions as they should be. This is attributed to their work. I have written the OC on this matter. Attended a Grooming Competition at Horse Lines of 2/5 Duke of Wellington. After the awards to man employed & competitor the points on which the successful competitors had secured.	8TN
"	3.5.18		Visited inspected the animals of No. 1 & 2 Section D.A.C. & Divisional Signal Company	8TN
"	4.5.18		Visited inspected animals for innovation in ThoR) M.I.5 Attended a conference at S.O.V.S. office II Corps. Visited inspected The animals of 185th Infantry Brigade, 460 Company R.E., 2/1 (1st WR) Field Ambulance and 455/A Company A.S.C.	8TN
"	5.5.18		Inspected the animals of 184 Infantry Brigade, 460 Company R.E. No 3 Section D.A.C. Divisional Signal Company and Divisional HQuarters	8TN

WAR DIARY / INTELLIGENCE SUMMARY

Army Form C. 2118.

A.D.M.S. 62nd (2nd) Division

Place	Date	Hour	Summary of Events and Information	Remarks and references to Appendices
Arthel	6.5.18		Visited and inspected the animals of the following units (y. M. H., Y.S.(M.G.) Field Ambulances 437th Company R.E. and Divisional Machine Gun Battalion. Handed a transfer list to the 186th Infantry Brigade	62D
"	7.5.18		Visited inspected the animals for evacuation on M.O.R.s to b.s. Inspected the animals of 55th, 53d, 57th & 578th Company A.S.C.	5th
"	8.5.18		Visited and inspected the animals in the 3.0 & 2/2 Brigades R.F.A. and the 9 & 29 Durham Pioneers Battalion. The train roads of the first two days are eighth, were not ended to improve the condition of the Horse animals in 61st Brigade, however I am satisfied they are not having anything. 2nd H. Brigade are not looking quite as well as they are on my last visit.	62D
"	9.5.18		Visited and inspected the animals of 187 X Infantry Brigade. M.M.P. Divisional Anjant Company and 46 Company R.E.	5th
"	10.5.18		Visited inspected animals of the 185th X Infantry Brigade. 461st Company R.S. and 55th Company A.S.C.	62D
"	11.5.18		Attended a conference at M.O.V.S. Office in Corps. Visited Transported off. 461 Field Ambulance animals. Visited inspected an animal at the H. of H.L.G.th suffering from a disease resembling Gen.	

Army Form C. 2118.

Original

WAR DIARY
or
INTELLIGENCE SUMMARY.
(Erase heading not required.)

D.A.D.V.S. 62nd (2nd) Division

Instructions regarding War Diaries and Intelligence Summaries are contained in F. S. Regs., Part II. and the Staff Manual respectively. Title pages will be prepared in manuscript.

Place	Date	Hour	Summary of Events and Information	Remarks and references to Appendices
Methil	*Continued*			
	11.5.18		Epizootic Lymphangitis. Two animals were sent to M.V.S. and inoculations given for others to be taken forwards to No 8 Veterinary Hospital for microscopic examination. Visited & inspected on arrival at 51/3 K Company H.T.C. suspects of Epizootic Lymphangitis. The animal was removed to M.V.S. inoculations from five horses to be taken forwards for microscopic examination.	D.D.V.S. 65th Div.
	12.5.18		Visited and inspected the animals of 310 T. Br. 1 Brigade R.F.A. Visited H.Q.s R.F.A. R.V.S. 88th Reconnoissance the A.D.V.S. & Staff Officers of the corps during their inspection of the animals of 310 T.Br. 1 Brigade R.F.A. The A.D.V.S. visited the D.A.F.	66th
	13.5.18		Inspects the sick cases of Suspected Epizootic Lymphangitis.	66th
	14.5.18		Inspects the animals of No.1 & 3 Sections D.A.C. The 5/6 & 7/3 (6th) Field Ambulances. 18th L Infantry Brigade and 460 K Company R.F.	18th L 55th
	15.5.18		Visits & inspects remounts at Engineered. Inspects the animals belonging to the following units. 186 A Infantry Brigade. The Anchors Inn Battalion. 457 K Company R.E. The D.A.V.S. Visits the M.V.S. & inspects the cases of suspected Epizootic Lymphangitis.	55th
	16.5.18		Visits & inspects the animals of 310 T.Br. 1 Brigade R.F.A. and 7/3 (6th) Field Ambulance. The six cases of Suspected Epizootic Lymphangitis have been declared negative by microscopic examination.	D.F.

Army Form C. 2118.

WAR DIARY
of
INTELLIGENCE SUMMARY.
(Erase heading not required.)

Instructions regarding War Diaries and Intelligence Summaries are contained in F. S. Regs., Part II. and the Staff Manual respectively. Title pages will be prepared in manuscript.

Original

DADVS 62nd (2nd WR) Division

Place	Date	Hour	Summary of Events and Information	Remarks and references to Appendices
[?]	17.5.18		Inspected horses & mules of Corps. Visited 2/1 (WR) mobile Veterinary Section	83/1
"	18.5.18		Visited and inspected the animals of the following units, 185th & 186th Infantry Brigades. 2/1 & 2/2 WR Field Ambulances.	83/1
"	19.5.18		Visited 2/1 (WR) Mobile Veterinary Section. Visited & inspected the animals in the following units, 451st & 460th Companies R.E. 63rd Divisional Machine Gun Battalion. No 3 Section D.A.C. & Mobile Veterinary Section 62nd	83/1
"	20.5.18		Visited & inspected the animals of Divisional Head Quarters, Signal Depot Company and 164th Infantry Brigade.	83/1
"	21.5.18		Visited & inspected animals of No 1 & 2 Section D.A.C. Inspected animals of 2/3rd. 296th Bde. S.A.A. Division. Visited 2/1 (WR) Mobile Veterinary Section.	83/1, 83/10
"	22.5.18		Visited & inspected the animals of 305 & 312 N Brigades R.F.A. and 525 Company A.S.C. Visited 2/1 (WR) M.V.S.	83/1
"	23.5.18		Inspected the animals of Divisional Head Quarters, Signal Company. No 3 Section D.A.C. and Visited 2/1 (WR) M.V.S.	83/1, 83/10
"	24.5.18		Inspected animals in 310 & 313th Brigades R.F.A.	83/1
"	25.5.18		Visited & inspected the animals of 186th Infantry Brigade. Attended a conference at ADVS Office in Corps HQ	83/1
"	26.5.18		Visited & inspected animals of No 3 Section D.A.C. Divisional Machine Gun Battalion & 185th Infantry Brigade. Visited Mobile Veterinary Section	83/1

Army Form C. 2118.

WAR DIARY
or
INTELLIGENCE SUMMARY.
(Erase heading not required.)

Original

Instructions regarding War Diaries and Intelligence Summaries are contained in F. S. Regs., Part II. and the Staff Manual respectively. Title pages will be prepared in manuscript.

D.A.D.V.S. 62nd (2/2nd R) Division

Place	Date	Hour	Summary of Events and Information	Remarks and references to Appendices
La en Action	17.5.19		Visits & inspects the animals of the following units viz. 2/1 & 2/2nd R1 Field Ambulances, 9th Durham Lancer Battalion.	FBB
	18.5.19		Visits & inspects the animals in the 187th Infantry Brigade. Visits & inspects the animals in the following units viz. 3/1, 3/2 & 3/3 R1, & 2/1 & 2/2 R1 Companies Divisional Train, 3rd, 4th and 5th Sections R.A.C., 2/2 & 2/3 Field Ambulance & 2/1 (2/2R) M.V.S.	FBB
	19.5.19		Visits & inspects the animals of 310th & 311th F Brigades R.S.A. & 462nd Mobile Veterinary Section. The animals in 306 Brigade and in fair condition. Clothing fits and in good condition. Those of 311 F Brigade show signs of improvement, but are far from satisfactory, particularly B & D Batteries.	FBB
	20.5.19		Visits the 9/10th Mobile Veterinary Section. Visits & inspects the animals of the following units 185 and 186th Infantry Brigades. Divisional Signal Company, 9th Durham Pioneers and 461 Company R.E.	FBB
	21.5.19		Visits & inspects the animals of the 187th Infantry Brigade, 457 & 460 Companies R.E., 2/1 & 2/2 Field Ambulance & 2/1(2/2R) Mobile Veterinary Section.	FBB

F. O'Neill Major A.V.C.
D.A.D.V.S. 62/2/2R Division

14

Original

Vol 18

Confidential

War Diary
of
D.A.D.S. & T. 2nd (AUS) Div

From 1/6/18
To 30/6/18

Vol: XVIII

Army Form C. 2118.

Original

WAR DIARY
or
INTELLIGENCE SUMMARY.

(Erase heading not required.)

A.D.V.S. 62nd (2/1st) Division

Instructions regarding War Diaries and Intelligence Summaries are contained in F.S. Regs., Part II. and the Staff Manual respectively. Title pages will be prepared in manuscript.

Place	Date	Hour	Summary of Events and Information	Remarks and references to Appendices
Queen Anne's Mansions	1.6.18		Visited and inspected the animals of 310th & 312th Brigades R.F.A. and 2/1 (2/4th) Mobile Veterinary Section. There is a marked improvement in the animals of 311th Brigade	
"	2.6.18		Inspected the animals of the following units 73rd, 63rd Divisional Machine Gun Battalion, No 3 Section 65th D.A.C., 2/1, 2/2 (206th) Field Ambulance, Divisional Supply Company, Head Quarters and 2/1, 6/8, 7/8, N.F.	68%
"	3.6.18		Inspected the animals of the 183rd & 186th Infantry Brigades, 461 Company R.E. 2/1st Queens Own Hussars, 2/1 (187) Mobile Veterinary Section, 2/5 West Riding Service Battalion.	68%
"	4.6.18		Visited and inspected the animals of the 169th Infantry Brigade 457 & 460 Companies R.E. 525 R 512 & 537 T.S. & B. Companies Divisional Train and Mobile Veterinary Section.	68%
"	5.6.18		Visited and inspected the animals of 310 & 312 Brigade R.F.A. and 2/1 (2/4) Mobile Veterinary Section.	68%
"	6.6.18		Held a conference of Veterinary Officers. Visits inspected the animals of 65th No 1 and 2 section D.A.C. and 2/1 (168) Mobile Veterinary Section.	68%
"	7.6.18		Inspected the animals of Divisional Head Quarters, Supply Company, 2/1 7/8 Field Ambulance, 165th Infantry Brigade, and 458 Company R.E.	68%
"	8.6.18		Attended Conference at A.D.V.S. offices Le Touret. Visits inspected the animals of 536, 53 & 538 Companies R.S.C. 7/3 Field Ambulance.	68%

Original

WAR DIARY
of
INTELLIGENCE SUMMARY.
(Erase heading not required.)

Army Form C. 2118.

A.T.V.S 64rd (H.R.) Division

Place	Date	Hour	Summary of Events and Information	Remarks and references to Appendices
Div. an H.Qrs	8.6.18		Visited & inspected the animals of the 1/5 Devonshire Regiment & 7/h Hampshire Regiment.	
			Got some of mange forces in each of these units. All the animals in these units Mallein tested. Visited 31(65R) Mobile Veterinary Station.	
"	9.6.18		Inspected the animals Mallein tested in the 1/5 Devon & 7/h Hampshire Regiments	65/8
"	10.6.18		Visited the 31(64R) Mobile Veterinary Section. Visited and inspected the animals of Divisional Signal Company and Headquarters Ammunition Batallion. Inspected the animals of 595th Brigade R.F.A. 59th Division attached to 63rd Division. Visited 31(65R) M.V.S	65/10
"	11.6.18		Visited & inspected the animals of the following units:- 1/9 Py K.R Infantry Brigade 453, 7 460 ? Companies R.F. 9 & Divisions, 9/2/6 R Royal Scots & Mobile Veterinary Station.	65/11
"	12.6.18		Visited & inspected the animals of 310 & 315 K Brigade R.F.A. and 555, 556, 557, 558, Companies A.S.C.	65/12
"	13.6.18		Held Weekly Conference of all V.O's attached Inspected the animals of N° 1 & Lectures R.A.C. Visited 31(65R) Mobile Veterinary Station.	65/13
"	14.6.18		Visited & inspected the animals of Veterinary and A.G Divisional Head Quarters Signal Company, Section Linears, N°3 Section R.A.C. & N° 5 Field Ambulance, 188 K Infantry Brigade, Indian Linear.	65/14

Army Form C. 2118.

WAR DIARY
or
INTELLIGENCE SUMMARY.
(Erase heading not required.)

D.A.D.V.S. 62nd (2/A) Division

Instructions regarding War Diaries and Intelligence Summaries are contained in F.S. Regs., Part II. and the Staff Manual respectively. Title pages will be prepared in manuscript.

Place	Date	Hour	Summary of Events and Information	Remarks and references to Appendices
Queen Croton	15.6.18		Attended a conference at A.D.V.S. Office & Open. Visited & inspected the animals of Divisional Reserve Gun Battalion and No.(2/A) Mobile Veterinary Section	S/R
"	16.6.18		Visited and inspected the animals of the following Infantry Brigades 185th, 186th & 187th. Inspects the Mobile Veterinary Section	S/R
"	17.6.18		Inspects the animals of the Household Regiment & remounts in enroute horse B. Depots	S/R
"	18.6.18		Inspects the animals of 310 & 311 Brigades R.F.A. Visits Sphere M.V.S. Visits and inspects the animals of the following units 1/3 457 & 460 & 461 Companies R.E. 1/5 Devons & West Yorks. Visits the 2/1(62.d) 2/2 & 2/3 remounts M.M. & horses	S/R
"	19.6.18		Inspects the animals of Divisional Reserve Gun Battalion, No.3 Section D.T.C. The 2/1 & 2/4 Field Ambulances and Divisional Head Quarters. Visits 2/1(62.d) M.V.S.	S/R
"	20.6.18		Held a Conference of Veterinary Officers. Visited and inspected the animals in Nº.72 Section D.T.C.1 and 2/1(62.d) M.V.S.	S/R
"	21.6.18		Visits & inspects the animals in the following units 1/3 186th Infantry Brigade 457 Company R.E. 1/5 Devons, 8 West Yorks, and 9th Durham Pioneers. Visits 2/1(62.d) M.V.S.	S/R
"	22.6.18		Attended a conference at A.D.V.S. Office II Corps. Visits 535 Company R.E. 2 M.V.S.	S/R

WAR DIARY of INTELLIGENCE SUMMARY.

Army Form C. 2118.

A.D.M.S. 62 (W.R.) Division

Place	Date	Hour	Summary of Events and Information	Remarks and references to Appendices
Sec. en Caloies	23.6.18		Inspected the animals of Divisional Hodrs. Ein Battalion, q.F. Dvision Reserve 185th Infantry Brigade. 1/1 & 1/3 Field Ambulance. Forties The M(OR) M.V.S	68/12
"	24.6.18		Visited and inspected the animals of 310 & 311th Brigades R.F.A & 1/1 (W.R) M.V.S	68/12
"	25.6.18		Divisional units moving into a new area.	68/12
"	26.6.18		Head Quarters. Signals & 1/1(W.R) M.V.S. Visited & inspected the animals of the following units Viz. 306th Brigade R.F.A. 185th Infantry Brigade 1/3 Field Ambulance, 515 & 516 Coys. A.S.C & 1/1(W.R) M.V.S	68/12
"	27.6.18		Inspected the animals of 187th Infantry Brigade. 1/2 (W.R) Field Ambulance. 1/4 Hampshire Regiment. 1/4 Duke of Wellington's Company machine Gun Battalion 1/1 (W.R) M.V.S	68/12
"	28.6.18		Visited & inspected animals of 311st Brigade R.F.A 1/1(W.R) Field Ambulance O.A.C 1/1(W.R) Field Ambulance. 1/5 Devons. 460 Company R.E. ? Ports Veterinary Section.	68/12
"	29.6.18		Attended Conference at A.D.V.S Office IV Corps. Went to Lycee and to inspect remains C. Visited 1/1(W.R) M.V.S	68/12
"	30.6.18		Inspected the animals of the following units. Viz 187th Infantry Brigade. Ord Company M.G. Battalion. 2/5 (W.R.) Field Ambulance. 2/4 Duke of Wellington's. 1/4 Hampshires. 1/1 M.V.S.	68/12

24

Original

Confidential
War Diary
D. D. & D. 21. L.
Col. (H.R.) Greiner
Thos. H.R. Greiner

From 1-7-17
To 31-7-17

VR 19

Original

Army Form C. 2118.

WAR DIARY
or
INTELLIGENCE SUMMARY.
(Erase heading not required.)

Army Troops 66 (2nd E.R.) Division

Instructions regarding War Diaries and Intelligence Summaries are contained in F. S. Regs., Part II. and the Staff Manual respectively. Title pages will be prepared in manuscript.

Place	Date	Hour	Summary of Events and Information	Remarks and references to Appendices
Gen. on Active	1.7.18		Visited and inspected the animals of 310th Brigade R.F.A. 2/(66R) Field Ambulance	
"	2.7.18		2/5 Stores of Wellington & 2/(66R) M.T.S. Visits and inspects the animals of the 331st Brigade R.F.A. 3rd Section D.A.C. "B" Section 55th Company H.Q.C and 2/(66R) M.T.S.	66R
"	3.7.18		Inspects the animals of Divisional Signal Company C. Company A.S.B. 55 R+52 R Company F.C. Divisional Head Quarters & 2/(66R) M.T.S.	66R
"	4.7.18		Inspects the animals in the following lines W/2 A Company A.S.C. 8th Yard Forks 2/3(66R) Field Ambulance, 55 H Company R.E.C., 2/5 West Yorks 9th Durham	66R
"	5.7.18		Grenoss 7/(66R) F.A.S. Visits & inspects the animals in the following W/443 2/(66R) Field Ambulance 2/5 Stores of Wellington 457 H Company R.E. B+C+D+F 2/7 (66R) M.T.S.	66R
"	6.7.18		Attended conference at A.D.V.S. II Corps. Visits and inspects the animals of the following units W/2 461 Company R.E. 2/5 (66R) Field Ambulance 2/4 Stores of Wellington 1 Company A.S. Battalion 2/4 Hampshires & 2/(66R) A.S.S	66R
"	7.7.18		Inspects the animals of 187 H Infantry Bde Signal Company, C Company A.S Battalion, and 1/1 58 72	
"	8.7.18		Inspects the animals of C Company A.S. Battalion 8th Yard Forks 2/3(66R) Field Ambulance, 9th Durhams and 2/(66R) M.T.S.	66R

Army Form C. 2118.

Original

WAR DIARY
or
INTELLIGENCE SUMMARY.
(Erase heading not required.)

Instructions regarding War Diaries and Intelligence Summaries are contained in F. S. Regs., Part II. and the Staff Manual respectively. Title pages will be prepared in manuscript.

A.T.O.V.S. 63rd (NR) Division

Place	Date	Hour	Summary of Events and Information	Remarks and references to Appendices
Sus. en Artois	9.7.18		Visited and inspected the animals of the H.Q's of the Divisional Signal Company and Divisional Headquarters. H(NR) D.V.S. 63rd D.S.C. Captain Thorn R.C. went on leave.	OTh.
"	10.7.18		Inspected the animals of 313th Brigade R.F.A. '15' Devons. 525 Company A.S.C. & M.T.	OTh.
"	11.7.18		Visited & inspected the animals in the following units: H(NR) Field Ambulance. H.Q. of H(NR) Infantry Brigade. B Company. M.G. Battalion. 189th Infantry Brigade.	OTh.
"	12.4.18		Inspected the animals of 52nd & 63rd Company A.S.C. H(NR) Divl Ambulance and H.Q. Divn of Wellington. Visited the Mobile Veterinary Section.	OTh.
"	13.7.18		Visited & inspected the animals of the 63rd Infantry Brigade. Made arrangements to evacuate all animals in the Division unable to travel, preparatory to the Division moving to a new area.	OTh.
"	14.7.18		Standing by ready to move. Visited the H(NR) D.V.S.	OTh.
"	15.7.18		Left Div en letters and entrained the Divisional transport at Mondicourt 4.30 am. All this day on rail.	OTh.
Smith le Camp	16.7.18		Arrived at Smithley le Camp (Area 1) at 3.30 pm. Nothing of particular interest on the journey. All animals arrived in good condition. Parties to Brienne (Cholera) took personnel the night. The Mobile Vety Section arrived at Smithly le Camp.	OTh.

Army Form C. 2118.

Original

WAR DIARY
of
INTELLIGENCE SUMMARY.
(Erase heading not required.)

A.D.V.S. 65th(?) Division

Instructions regarding War Diaries and Intelligence Summaries are contained in F. S. Regs., Part II. and the Staff Manual respectively. Title pages will be prepared in manuscript.

Place	Date	Hour	Summary of Events and Information	Remarks and references to Appendices
Trunes	17.7.18		Received from France Two Trench mean. Visits the A.V.C. XVII Corps at Verlin.	AVR
Truns Chaps Terns	18.7.18		The M.V.S. arrives here after 4 days travel. Day the arrival of the following unit on the march 19 A.S.C. Battn 8th Brigade, 9th Durham. M + H(OR) Fees Ambulances. Bivouacked reached the Battalion 15 Devon. Reports Company, 53 & Company R.S.C. and animals of A.V.C. all the animals showing the strain of the long march well. No acompliments.	AVR
Yeres Aux Manx	19.7.18		Bivouacked truly. Moving forward. Visits YboW M.V.S	AVR
"	20.7.18		Public Veterinary lecture turned from Forver here seem to Givenne. Visits Mangrets No animals of No 3 Coden D.S.C. the M.V.S. in the last named place.	AVR
"	21.7.18		Visits and inspects at St Maign the animals of Divisional Headquarters, A, H. S. Headquarters. R.A. 8 West Yorks. 15 Devon	AVR
"	22.7.18		Visits and inspects the animals of Divisional Tram Hg 525. 536. 537 & 526 Company RASC	AVR
"	23.7.18		Visits the H.Q.S of Givenne and Ho 3 (note) A.T.C	AVR
"	24.7.18		Visits inspects animals of H^q > 1 3 Section D.C.L. 31st Brigade R.A.A & M(OR) M.V.S	AVR
"	"		Inspects the animals of 3th Brigade R.F.A	AVR

Army Form C. 2118.

WAR DIARY
of
INTELLIGENCE SUMMARY.
(Erase heading not required.)

Army of .... 63rd (R.N.) Division

Instructions regarding War Diaries and Intelligence Summaries are contained in F.S. Regs., Part II. and the Staff Manual respectively. Title pages will be prepared in manuscript.

Place	Date	Hour	Summary of Events and Information	Remarks and references to Appendices
Sous Lieut. Arvril St. 7.18			Visited the M.(B.R.) M.V.S. Had a Conference of Veterinary Officers.	
"			R.A.V.C. XXII Corps during his inspection of the animals of the following units. accompanied the V.3. M.(B.R.) M.V.S. Nos. 1, 2 & 3 Sections R.S.C. 310 Co. & 311 Brigades R.S.A.	63R
"	25.7.18		Visited M.(B.R.) M.V.S. Performed the routine duties. Heavy evacuation in animals of the Division due to bombing.	63R
"	26.7.18		Inspected animals of Divisional Head Quarters. Signal Company. 188th Infantry Brigade. Sanitary Section. exempt animals externes.	63R
"	27.7.18		Visited and inspected the animals of 457, 460 & 461st Companies R.E.	63R
"	28.7.18		Visited No. 3 Section R.A.S.C. Visited M.(B.R.) M.V.S. arranged for evacuation of evacuated wounded animals.	63R
"	29.7.18		Visited and inspected the animals of 315th Brigade R.F.A. and No. 2 & 3 (R.F.) Field Ambulance. Captain Elwood reports on his return from leave.	63R
"	30.7.18		Wrote the monthly reports in health & sanitation of the animals in the units of the Division. Divisional Artillery moved out. Visits animals. Divisional Head Quarters.	63R
"	31.7.18		Visited M.(B.R.) M.V.S. Made arrangements about sick wounded animals in case of a move. Visited sick and exempt animals. Supplied animals of the Signal Company R.A.F. G.E. &cc.	63R

E.C. Reid. Mayor. D.A.D.V.S. 63rd (R.N.) Division.

19 Original

Confidential

War Diary
of
D.A.D.S. 62nd (W.R) Divn

From 1~8~18
To 31~8~18

Vol: XX

Army Form C. 2118.

WAR DIARY
of
INTELLIGENCE SUMMARY.
(Erase heading not required.)

Instructions regarding War Diaries and Intelligence Summaries are contained in F. S. Regs., Part II. and the Staff Manual respectively. Title pages will be prepared in manuscript.

A.H.Q.R.S. 63rd (N.R.) Division

Place	Date	Hour	Summary of Events and Information	Remarks and references to Appendices
Sous le Vent	1.8.18		Made several Divisional Headquarters & made arrangements to move the H.Q.R.S. N.R.S. Ammn Office from Sous le Vent to Bracourt. H.(N.R.) N.R.S. moved from Germans to Bracourt. Inspected the arrivals of Signal Company Headquarters. R.J. & R.S.	
Bracourt	2.8.18		Visited and inspected the arrivals of 556, 558 & 556 Companies and 24 Hampshire Battalion, and the West of Wellington. These heavy draughts arrived of the last draught and has been during the early morning of the 2nd & 3rd. No leave were asking. 3 were heavy draughts arrived were very ill. The remainder were off their duties, but showed no symptoms of symptoms. The movement and conditions of the command were stiffness of movement intermittent spasms of the muscles came as seen in horses attempting to vomit. Temperature 105° pulse about imperceptible inspection of the buccaus membranes of the eye, respiratory slightly engorged. Horses cooled with moisture slight chary pain. The animals died after 36 hours from symptoms. On Post mortem. The heart was healthy but contained anti muscular clots. Liver, lungs, kidneys & kidneys healthy. Stomach slightly congested & contains a large quantity of engesta mixed with fluids.	

Army Form C. 2118.

WAR DIARY
or
INTELLIGENCE SUMMARY.
(Erase heading not required.)

Instructions regarding War Diaries and Intelligence Summaries are contained in F.S. Regs., Part II. and the Staff Manual respectively. Title pages will be prepared in manuscript.

2/4 D.Y.L.S. 62nd Bde, Division

Place	Date	Hour	Summary of Events and Information	Remarks and references to Appendices
Beauval	2.8.18		The large barn contains a large quantity of ingrets & petrofleurs, there are various inflammation of this copse. Heavy Zeppelin raid by inscriptions processed to Beauval & informed the A.D.F.S. XXII Corps of the outrage. He acknowledged the orders received, the moment the Vickers of the arms case, I made arrangement to send him to following day at 10.30 a.m.	[signature]
	3.8.18		Rest. A.D.F.S. XXII Corps at the horse lines. Brozelley so arranged. No further deaths has occurred during the night. There was a slight improvement in front of the animals. There were 3 heavy draughts, animals that were Caseshoes not safe to enter, arrangements were made to leave them to T.D.F.S. XXII Corps. Caught State that the Cranage is forwarded from 2 D.O.V.S XXII Corps. have written my report of this damage so in my opinion this to some extent in the hand kept perfectly in the horses care. Same was been removed that out of this animal numbered above as unfit. I hoped has since died. Left Beauval proceeded to Epernay for internment. No details informant of Vickers left in same state and arrived at Vertus. O Down took the 8P and	[signature]

T2134. Wt. W708-776. 500000. 4/15. Sir J. C. & S.

Army Form C. 2118.

WAR DIARY
OF
INTELLIGENCE SUMMARY.
(Erase heading not required.)

2nd ??? 62nd ???? Division

Place	Date	Hour	Summary of Events and Information	Remarks and references to Appendices
Can en ?????	5.8.18		Arrived and detrained at Andruicq and Proceeded to Rangeville at Bos-en-Artois	
			The 2/10th A.V.S. detrained at Candas & proceeded to Carton carrying this the	
			same night	5??
	6.8.18		Visited and inspected the animals of the following units - The Machine Gun Battalion	
			505 & 506 Companies R.E. - 313 Station D.A.C. Engineer Company R.H.Q. and	
			With Infantry Brigade. All the animals of the 2nd Duke of Wellingtons had been	
			off their feet & were now almost recovered and I do not anticipate any more trouble	5??
			Visited & inspected the animals of the following units 2/1 & 7/2 (6?R) Fiel Ambulances	
	7.8.18		103rd Infantry Brigade and 313rd Engineer R.H.Q. The animals of the 8/? look	
			9/15 Devons have fired off in condition exceedingly. and Horses of B & D Batteries	
			313 Brigade are very unsatisfactory. All these animals have had a fairly strenuous	
			time for the good time ????? Fort Scan and whilst at Evricourt the 13 shire how	
			Condition. Saw of Lt Spencer this is at a Res about taken on supping of the	
			animals of this unit.	5??
	8.8.18		Visited and inspected the animals of the following units -1/3, 36?? Brigade R.F.A. 2 & 3 Seaforths D.F.C.	
			The Durham Pioneers & 258 Company R.A.C. The animals in C & D Batteries 306 Bde have fallen off in	
			condition a good deal	5??

T2134. Wt. W708—776. 500000. 4/15. Sir J.C.&S.

Army Form C. 2118.

WAR DIARY
of
INTELLIGENCE SUMMARY.
(Erase heading not required.)

A.D.M.S. 62nd Division

Instructions regarding War Diaries and Intelligence Summaries are contained in F. S. Regs., Part II. and the Staff Manual respectively. Title pages will be prepared in manuscript.

Place	Date	Hour	Summary of Events and Information	Remarks and references to Appendices
In the Field	8.8.18		Visited and inspected the arrival of the following units viz 2/1 & 2/3 Field Ambulances also 15th West York 15th Durham 515 & 516 Companies A.S.C. and 457 Company R.E. the majority of the arrival in the Devons are in as fair a condition as they were 3 weeks ago but this are to the hard work during recent operations. Visited the 2/4 West Riding R.F.S.	68/R
			Inspected at Doullens the animals of the 2/6 London Regiment most these are on the thin side R.T.S	68/R
	10.8.18		Visited Probationers and inspected 150 remounts. The heavy draught are in good stamp. Light draught fair trades on the thin side	68/R
	11.8.18		Visited 2/4 W(est)R(iding) F.A. Inspected the animals of the following units viz 311 & 312 Brigades R.F.A. 463 & 461 Companies R.E. and 187 Infantry Brigade	58/R
	12.8.18		Visited, inspected the animals of the following units viz Divisional Headquarters and Signal Company 2/6 London Regiment 186 Infantry Brigade and Divisional Machine Gun Battalion	68/R
	13.8.18		Visited inspected the animals of the following units viz. 310 Brigade R.F.A. 515 & 516 Companies A.S.C. 457 Company R.E. 2/1(or R) Field Ambulance & 185th Infantry Brigade	68/R
	14.8.18		Visited the W(est)R(iding) R.F.A. Inspected the animals of 310 Brigade R.F.A. 9th Durham Pioneers 2/1(or R) Field Ambulances	68/R

T2134. Wt. W708-776. 500000. 4/15. Sir J. C. & S.

Army Form C. 2118.

WAR DIARY
of
INTELLIGENCE SUMMARY.
(Erase heading not required.)

D.A.D.V.S. 62nd (W.R.) Division

Instructions regarding War Diaries and Intelligence Summaries are contained in F.S. Regs., Part II. and the Staff Manual respectively. Title pages will be prepared in manuscript.

Place	Date	Hour	Summary of Events and Information	Remarks and references to Appendices
Authie	15.8.18		Moved from Sars en Artois to Authie.	SP6
"	16.8.18		Accompanied the A.D.V.S. IX Corps during his inspection of the animals of the following units :- 5/ 7th Hampshire Regiment. Divisional Machine Gun Battalion. 457 Company R.E. Visited inspected the animals of 187 & Stanley Infantry Brigade	SP6
"	17.8.18		Visited inspected the animals of 2/4 (W.R.) Field Ambulance and 7/(W.R.) M.T.S	SP6
"			H.Q. & Signal Company.	
"	18.8.18		Took over duties of D.A.D.V.S. vice Major Kells proceeding on leave to U.K. Visited and inspected animals on Divisional Head Quarters and 528 Coy A.S.C.	S.P.6.
Grenas.	19.8.18		Moved from Authie to Grenas. Visits and inspected animals of 186th Infantry Brigade	S.P.6.
"	20.8.18		Moved from Grenas to Bavincourt.	S.P.6.
Bavincourt	21.8.18		Moved from Bavincourt to Sullens. Inspected 327 Coy A.S.C., 2/3 W.R. Field Ambulance and 2/1 (W.R.) Field Ambulance.	S.P.6.
Sullens.	22.8.18		Received returns from Veterinary Officer. Visited & inspected animals on 9 Durham Light Infantry and 187 Infantry Brigade.	S.P.6.
"	23.8.18		Visited and inspected animals of F.A.Q. and 295 Coy A.S.C.	S.P.6.

Army Form C. 2118.

WAR DIARY
INTELLIGENCE SUMMARY.
(Erase heading not required.)

A.D.V.S. 62nd Division

Instructions regarding War Diaries and Intelligence Summaries are contained in F.S. Regs., Part II. and the Staff Manual respectively. Title pages will be prepared in manuscript.

Place	Date	Hour	Summary of Events and Information	Remarks and references to Appendices
Buicnvillers	24-8-18		Moved from Souliens to Buicnvillers. Visited 327 Coy. A.S.C. & M.V.S. and selected site for "advanced Veterinary Post".	D.R.C.
"	25-8-18		Visited and inspected 186th and 187th Infantry Brigades, S.A.A. section 62nd D.A.C. 62nd Machine gun Battalion, 9th Durham Light Infantry, 457, 460, 461 Coys. R.E. and D.H.Q. and 62nd Divisional Signal Coy. and M.G.R.E.	D.R.C.
"	26-8-18		Visited 2/3 (WR) Field Ambulance, and 2/1 (WR) field ambulance, and D.H.Q.	D.R.C.
"	27-8-18		Visited 186th Bde and 457 Coy R.E.	D.R.C.
"	28-8-18		Visited 187th Infantry Bde and 2/2 (WR) Field Ambulance, also 9, 461, 762nd Div Sig Coy	D.R.C.
"	29-8-18		Collected return A.F's A 2008 for wk. Visited 185th Infantry Brigade	D.R.C.
"	30-8-18		Visited 186th Infantry Brigade and HQ RA and HQ RE also S.A.A section 9 A.D. D.R.C.	D.R.C.
			Prepared monthly report for G.O.C. Division 2 A.D.V.S. " Corps.	
Douchy	31-8-18		Moved to Douchy. Visited Field Ambulances /62 Division & D.H.Q.	D.R.C.

J.R. Babb (GF)
F.R. nor.
Capt. nor.
a/S.A.D.V.S. 62 Division

19

Original

Vol. 21

Confidential

War Diary
of

R.A.V.S. 63rd (U.R.) Div.

From 1-9-18   Vol. XXI   To 30-9-18

Original

Army Form C. 2118.

WAR DIARY
or
INTELLIGENCE SUMMARY.
(Erase heading not required.)

D.A.D.V.S. 62nd (W.R.) Division

Instructions regarding War Diaries and Intelligence Summaries are contained in F. S. Regs., Part II. and the Staff Manual respectively. Title pages will be prepared in manuscript.

Place	Date	Hour	Summary of Events and Information	Remarks and references to Appendices
Doncly-la-Ayette	1-9-15		Inspected animals of 186th Infantry Bde., 9th Durham Light Infantry and 528 Coy. A.S.C.	5722
	2-9-18		Inspected animals of 185th Infantry Bde. 2/2 and 2/3 (WR) Field Ambulance	5726.
	3-9-18		Inspected animals of 187 Infantry Bde. and 2/1 (W.R.) Field Ambulance and 460 Coy. R.E. and D.H.Q.	5.R.E.
Courcelles	4.9.18		Reported for duty on return from leave 2/(WR) A/S moved from Doncly-la-Ayette to Courcelles (on the Courcelles-Sorricourt Road.). Visits the 2/(WR) M.V.S	58.R
	5.9.18		Visited and inspected the animals of the following units. 62 Divisional Headquarters, Signal Company, 457, 460, 461 Companies R.E. 186th Infantry Brigade, 9 Durham Pioneer Battalion, 2/1 & 2/2 (WR) Field Ambulance. The condition of nearly all the animals may be considered satisfactory except those of the Pioneer Battalion and a few an 457 & 461 Companies R.E.	58.A
	6.9.18		Inspected the animals of the 185th & 187th Infantry Brigades. 516, 517 & 528 Companies A.S.C Divisional Heavy Gun Battalion and 2/3 Field Ambulance. The animals of the 9/30 London Regiment + 15th Dragoons are still on the Thin side but should improve with the amount of grazing they are getting. Visits 2/(WR) M.V.S	58.R

Original

Army Form C. 2118.

WAR DIARY
or
INTELLIGENCE SUMMARY.
(Erase heading not required.)

D.A.D.V.S. 62 (2/WR) Division

Instructions regarding War Diaries and Intelligence Summaries are contained in F.S. Regs., Part II. and the Staff Manual respectively. Title pages will be prepared in manuscript.

Place	Date	Hour	Summary of Events and Information	Remarks and references to Appendices
Courcelles	7.9.18		Attended a Conference at A.D.V.S. Office at Sautz. Inspected the animals of No 3 Section 1/(2/5) V.H.O. Visits 1/(67R) M.V.S.	68%
"	8.9.18		Visited and inspected the animals of the following units viz. 185, 186, 187th Infantry Brigades, 1/1 & 72 Field Ambulance. No 1. Company R.E. and 2/(62R) for L.S. The Divisional Artillery arrived in this area.	68%
"	9.9.18		Visited and inspected the Animals of the following units. 1/3 Divisional Sans- Garois. Signal Company 1/(62R) Field Ambulance. 313 Brigade R.F.A. The majority of the animals in the last named unit have gone down in condition during recent operations. It is particularly noticeable on D Battery, to a lesser extent in C. Visits 1/(62R) M.V.S.	68%
"	10.9.18		Visited 2/(62R) M.V.S. The unit moved from Carcelles to Francourt. No inspections to day owing to movement. If unit to another area.	68%
"	11.9.18		Move from Carcelles to Francourt. Inspected the animals of No 1 & 2 Sections D.A.C. & 310th Brigade R.F.A. The animals of this Brigade have lost condition considerably the past three weeks. It is particularly noticeable in B. Battery. The cause of this is the heavy work during the recent advance, aggravated by the most decidedly irregularity in feeding & forage.	68%

Original

WAR DIARY
of
INTELLIGENCE SUMMARY.
(Erase heading not required.)

Army Form C. 2118.

F.A.D.V.S. 63rd (N.R.) Division

Place	Date	Hour	Summary of Events and Information	Remarks and references to Appendices
Frencourt	10.9.18		Inspected the animals in the H/(N.R.) M.T. Establishment on annual veterinary and foot in Velu Wood.	A.V.S.
"	12.9.18		The animals of the following units. Brig. H.Q. Infantry Brigade, 467. 460. 461 Companies R.E., 536. 557. 558 Companies D.A.C. and H/(N.R.) M.T. were visited and inspected. The arrival of 313 F Brigade R.F.A. Headquarters and Nos Section D.A.C. H/(N.R.) Field Ambulance and H/(N.R.) M.T.S.	A.V.S.
"	13.9.18		Visits the Advance Veterinary Aid Post.	A.V.S.
"	14.9.18		Inspected the animals of the following units. Brig. H.Q. 467. 460. 461 Companies R.E. 188 F Infantry Brigade. 535 Company H.Q. Visits the Advance Veterinary Aid Post.	A.V.S.
Gomiecourt	15.9.18		Visits and inspects the animals of 310 F Brigade R.F.A. 555 Company R.G. and H (N.R) M.T. Arranged for 310 F Brigade horse lines to be taken over by H.O. Moved from Frencourt to Gomiecourt. H/(N.R) Mobile Veterinary Section moved from Frencourt to Gomiecourt.	A.V.S.
"	16.9.18		Visited and inspected the animals of the following units. 180 F. 190 F. Infantry Brigade. Divisional Troops F.A.S.C. Section H/(N.R) E.L. Station H/>76(N.R) Field Ambulance.	A.V.S.
"	17.9.18		Visits and inspects the animals. F 586. 557. 558 F Companies Divisional Train and H (N.R) M.T.S. The Director General of Veterinary Services was expected to arrive.	A.V.S.
"	18.9.18		Visit the Mobile Section. But being present for time was unable to do so.	A.V.S.

Army Form C. 2118.

Original WAR DIARY OF INTELLIGENCE SUMMARY.

(Erase heading not required.)

D.A.D.V.S. 62nd Division

Instructions regarding War Diaries and Intelligence Summaries are contained in F. S. Regs., Part II. and the Staff Manual respectively. Title pages will be prepared in manuscript.

Place	Date	Hour	Summary of Events and Information	Remarks and references to Appendices
Gomiecourt	19.9.18		Held a conference of Veterinary Officers. Visited and inspected the animals of the following units: 187th Infantry Brigade, 73 Field Ambulance and 71(WR) M.T.S.	OBM
"	20.9.18		Visited and inspected the animals of the 1/5 K.Y.L. Regiment, 1/5 Devons, 9th Durham Pioneers, 1/1 & 1/2 (WR) Field Ambulances & 71(WR) M.T.S.	OBM
"	21.9.18		Divisional Headquarters, Headquarters R.A. and Signal Company. Attended a Conference at A.D.V.S. Office VI Corps. Visited inspected and reported the animals of 526 & 527 & 528 T Companies R.E. and 71 (WR) M.T.S.	OBM
"	22.9.18		Visited and inspected the animals of Headquarters A, B, C & D Companies 9th Durham Pioneers 9th Durham Light Inf Battalion, 71(WR) M.T.S.	OBM
"	23.9.18		Inspected the animals of the following units viz 457, 458, 460, 461 Companies R.E. Nos 1 & 2 Western D.A.C. 553 Company A.S.C. & 71(WR) M.T.S.	OBM
"	24.9.18		Inspected the animals of the following units 103 Eastern D.A.C. 310 & 312 Th Brigades R.F.A. 9th Durham Pioneers and 1/5 Devons. There is an improvement in the appearance generally of the animals of 310 & 312 T Bde R.F.A. due partly to better supervision, evacuation of thin animals. Having an officer constantly at the Wagon Lines & Reed Battery. The condition of animals in 310 T Brigade has fallen off considerably. This is in my opinion accounted for by everyone being absent in front of Battery Wagon Lines & Reed Battery of Proper Supervision.	OBM

(A7093) Wt. W12595/M1275. 75,000. 1/17. D. D. & L., Ltd. Forms/C2118/14.

Army Form C. 2118.

Original

WAR DIARY
of
INTELLIGENCE SUMMARY.
(Erase heading not required.)

D.T.D.V.S. 62nd Division

Place	Date	Hour	Summary of Events and Information	Remarks and references to Appendices
Vancourt	25.9.18		Visits: H(WR), M.O.S and inspected arranged for accommodation, arranging for Division to move forward to P.13.a & b. Started an advance and started I.36.a (Sheet 57(c)) approximately the ammunition of the 187 Infantry Brigade.	
"	26.9.18		Analysis the arrival of the following units: 63 Signal Company, 556, 557 y 558 Companies A.S.C. 187th Infantry Brigade. H.O.S moved to site an annex rest billettes to Division and prior to these arriving.	MM
"	27.9.18		Visits: The H(WR), M.O.S and arranged aid post, evacuating the wound of 505 Company A.S.C. No. 1 Section D.A.C. & 75 Field Ambulance.	MM
"	28.9.18		Attended conference at A.D.M.S Hrs II Corps. With another officer to reconnoitre country recently taken, got the arrival of 73 Division.	MM
"	29.9.18		Visits: The H(WR) M.O.S and advance Veterinary aid post. Inspect the arrival of the following units (63rd), 555, 556, 558 Companies A.S.C and 182 & 183 Infantry Brigade. The 75 Section Reynold arrived as not leaving till tomorrow morning were been accommodate and attacks.	MM
"	30.9.18		The M.O.S moved yesterday to I.36 a.3 advance aid kitchen transferred at I.36 a (Sheet 57(c)) North M.O.S operated on annexes of 187 Infantry Brigade & 75 (HW) field Ambulance. The trouble is evacuate the Dam creatively from the Hurth they now look after all Divisions to be annoyed of the Artillery	

Lt Col Willson ADC ADMS 62nd Division

Original

No 23

Confidential
War Diary
of
H.Q.A.D.V.S. 62nd (wk) Divn:

From 1-10-18   To   31-10-18

Vol: XVII / XXII

Army Form C. 2118.

Original

WAR DIARY
or
INTELLIGENCE SUMMARY.

(Erase heading not required.)

Instructions regarding War Diaries and Intelligence Summaries are contained in F.S. Regs., Part II. and the Staff Manual respectively. Title pages will be prepared in manuscript.

D.A.D.V.S. 62nd (W.R.) Division

Place	Date	Hour	Summary of Events and Information	Remarks and references to Appendices
Gomiecourt	1/10/18		Visited 2/1 (W.R.) M.V.S. at Hermies and advanced Veterinary Aid Post at Havrincourt. Visited inspected the animals of 313th Brigade R.F.A. On the whole the animals in this Brigade are hard working then condition fairly good. Every Gunlett examined. The wastage remains high and there has also been a number of debility cases examined.	68%
"	2/10/18		Visited and inspected the animals in the following units viz 186th Infantry Brigade, 467, 460, 461 Companies R.E. 525, 526, 527 Companies R.A.S.C. R.A.C. and 2/1 (W.R.) M.V.S.	68%
"	3/10/18		Held a conference of V.O's Visited 2/1 (W.R.) M.V.S. Inspected the animals of 525, 526, 527 r 461 Companies A.S.C.	68%
Gomiecourt	4/10/18		Moved from Gomiecourt to Fermies. Inspected the animals in the following units Viz 185th Infantry Brigade, 75(W.R.) Field Ambulance and 2/1(67th) M.V.S.	68%
"	5/10/18		Inspection the animals of 312th Brigade R.F.A, B & D Batteries 310th Brigade R.F.A. 525th Company A.S.C. and 2/1 (W.R.) M.V.S. The condition of the animals in the three Batteries of 310th Brigade R.F.A. is most unsatisfactory, after many of them are rapidly reaching the debility stage, there are several factors contributory to this state of affairs, such as continuous hard work for a long period without rest, inadequate supply of water, insufficient field or forage and in addition to the foregoing lack of horses in Wittlerungenad irregularity in feeding. Generally unsatisfactory.	R.R.N.
"	6/10/18		Visited inspected the animals of 2/1(W.R.) R.V.S. Divisional Signal Company, 186th Infantry Brigade, 457, 460, 461 Companies R.E. and 2/1(W.R.) Field Ambulance.	68%

(A7092) Wt W2859/M1293. 75,000. 1/17. D.D. & L., Ltd. Forms/C:2118/14.

Original

Army Form C. 2118.

Instructions regarding War Diaries and Intelligence Summaries are contained in F. S. Regs., Part II. and the Staff Manual respectively. Title pages will be prepared in manuscript.

WAR DIARY
or
INTELLIGENCE SUMMARY.
(Erase heading not required.)

A.D.M.S. 62nd (W.R.) Division

Place	Date	Hour	Summary of Events and Information	Remarks and references to Appendices
Havrincourt	7/10/18		Visited and inspected the animals in the following units: Hd Qrs Section D.A.C, 62nd Divisional Mobile Vet. Section, 73 Field Ambulance, 526 & 578 Companies A.S.C, 185th Machine Gun Battalion and Y(W.R) M.G.B.	68½
"	8/10/18		Visited and inspected the animals for evacuation in the M(W.R) M.V.S. Parked and inspected the animals in the following units: 113, 91st Hardian Section, No 1, 2 sections R.H.Q. 326 Company A.S.C and A Battery 313 Brigade R.F.A. Received a list of 29 H.S. horses to go on the 9th and requested Hqrs. to arrange to evacuate these from Havrincourt.	68½
Havrincourt	9/10/18		Went to Hargincourt, the M(W.R) M.V.S. moved from Hermes to Hargincourt brought the animals of Divisional Headquarters, light Hargincourt, 187th Infantry Brigade Headquarters, to the locations of 312th & 311th Brigade R.F.A. not occupied and them to the location of 312th Brigade R.F.A.	68½
Havrincourt	10/10/18		The 311(W.R) M.V.S. moved from Hargincourt to Havrincourt. This Officer moved from Hargincourt to Havrincourt. Is all ranks of the Division were on the move and unable to parade and of the animals. Endeavoured to find the artillery units but as they had moved during the day was unable to locate them. Visited the Y(W.R) M.V.S. Casualties arranged Artillery units have been very this week and frequently I searched 313 Brigade R.F.A. is increasing. This is due to the fact that they have been subjected to a consideration extra use of great magnitude, according for by the fact that they have been unhorses by a number of engagements and the troop horses continuously have a long front and often there has been a scarcity of grain. Seven of the openmen are debility even in the new due to the extraordinary.	
Etroeul	11/10/18		Moved from Havrincourt to Etroeul. The Y(W.R) M.V.S. moves from Havrincourt to Y, 19, ES.0 Sheet 57B. Inspected the animals of 313 Brigade R.F.A. Divisional Machine Gun Battalion, 461 & 1059 Companies R.E. The animals in 315th Brigade R.F.A. are looking better than those of 313th Brigade. There are a number of animals in B.C. & D Batteries which respect not otherwise. They will have to be evacuated for debility.	68½

Army Form C. 2118.

WAR DIARY
of
INTELLIGENCE SUMMARY.
(Erase heading not required.)

Instructions regarding War Diaries and Intelligence Summaries are contained in F.S. Regs., Part II. and the Staff Manual respectively. Title pages will be prepared in manuscript.

A.D.M.S. 63rd (2nd) Division

Place	Date	Hour	Summary of Events and Information	Remarks and references to Appendices
Estaires	12/10/18		Attended a conference at A.D.M.S. Office II Corps. Tractors were engaged to take the animals in the following units. 1/9 186th Infantry Brigade 3(pdA) Field Ambulance 5 mineral headquarters to attend A.B.&C.	G.F.R.
"	13/10/18		Inspected the animals of 310th Brigade R.F.A. 525th Company A.S.C. 73 (2nd) Field Ambulance and 186th Infantry Brigade. The animals of 310th Brigade R.F.A. are slightly improved in condition, this is most noticeable in the case of D Battery. There are still a number of thin animals which will have to be evacuated when they obtain a rest. There are no thin horses in A, B, & C batteries.	G.F.R.
"	14/10/18		Inspected and investigated the animals of the following units viz 311th Brigade R.F.A., M.T. Section, D.A.C., 525 & 512 Companies A.S.C. and 4(pdA) M.T.T. Company 311th Brigade R.F.A. has an increase in sick animals. & Conditions of animal. The 311 Brigade is meeting this force - the batteries are opportunity to Graze them	G.F.R.
"	15/10/18		Tractors expedite the animals of the following units. 4/3 310th Brigade R.F.A. 155th Infantry Brigade A.B.&C Companies Machine Gun Battalion and Signal Company. Selected a site for mobile Veterinary Section at Grand Ennetières. The animals in the 1/10 London Regiment show a satisfactory improvement since last week. 310th Brigade have come out to rest. This will give the Battery Commanders an opportunity of grazing their thin animals & the rest will materially assist in the recuperation. Inspected the animals of the following units 93 1864 Infantry Brigade. 75(4BR) Field Ambulance 525th Company A.S.C. Public 5(pdA) Tn.15 at Trencey Farm. These were moved to-day from 23/19 C 50 Sheet 5y. 23 to the above named farm.	G.F.R.
"	16/10/18			G.F.R.

WAR DIARY
INTELLIGENCE SUMMARY

Army Form C. 2118.

D.A.D.V.S. 62nd (2nd) Division

Place	Date	Hour	Summary of Events and Information	Remarks and references to Appendices
Estouvennes	17/10/18		Visits and inspection the animals of 310 & 312th Brigades R.F.A. & M.T. M.T. The animals in both Brigades of Artillery shew an improvement in condition particularly 312.	657a
Beaulieu	18/10/18		Moved from Estouvennes to Beaulieu. Inspected the animals of the following units 185 of 186th Infantry Brigades. Nr. 1 & 2 Section D.A.C. Visited 2/1 (6-9) R.W.F.	657a
"	19/10/18		Attended conference at A.D.V.S. office IV Corps. Visited Stores (M.V.S. & the new Veterinary Col. G.H. Blenkinsop). Inspected the animals of the following units viz 525, 526 & 528 Company. A.S.C. M.T. 1/5 Field Ambulance and 187 Infantry Brigade.	657a
"	20/10/18		Horses removed for Divisional Artillery Veter. Hospital. M.3 Section D.A.C. 487 Company R.E.'s animals. Visits the same veterinary As. Col.	657a
"	21/10/18		Visited and inspected the animals of 310th Brigade. R.F.A. Visited the wagon lines of 312 Brigade R.F.A. the majority of animals were away working the guns & in two positions the evidence of the hard day's work is brought & most of them in the condition they are now possess. Visited some road horse to be secondary inspected the animals of 1/5 Cavalry Brigade Veterinary As. Col.	657a
"	22/10/18		Visited 1/1 & 2/1 (6-9) M.V.S. Inspected the animals of 185 & Infantry Brigade A & D Companies. 2nd Battalion Depot Company 2/1 m 1/3 Field Ambulance.	657a
"	23/10/18		Visited the same as Veterinary As. Col. Inspected the animals of the following units 1/3 - 3/4 Brigade R.F.A. 186 & Infantry Brigade B & C Company Divisional Machine Gun Battalion 408 & 461st Companies R.E. The general appearance of the animals in 3rd C Brigade is now much improved. No casualties among animals have been reported and Brigade are now able to fill up deficiencies. The animals in Machine Gun Battalion are numerically less and in condition although working very hard.	657a

Army Form C. 2118.

WAR DIARY
of
INTELLIGENCE SUMMARY.
(Erase heading not required.)

Army ... D.A.D.V.S. 63rd (N.R.) Division

Place	Date	Hour	Summary of Events and Information	Remarks and references to Appendices
Bovillers	24/10/18		Visited 4/N.F.A. Mobile Veterinary Section. Inspected the animals of 316, 317 & 318 Companies A.S.C., M.M.G. and 252nd R.I.F. Field Ambulance.	63/16
"	25/10/18		Visited Veterinary Mil. Set. Inspected the animals of 523rd Company A.S.C. and No. 1 & 2 Sections A.V.O. of 8th West Yorks.	63/16
"	26/10/18		Attended Conference at A.D.V.S. Office II Corps. Visited 4/N.F.A. Mobile Veterinary Section - Inspected the animals of the 183rd Infantry Brigade.	63/16
"	27/10/18		Visited & inspected the animals of 30 & 31 Brigades R.F.A and 4/N.F.A. Field Ambulance & "C" Battery 310? are loosing fairly well & there are very few animals to be evacuated. Those of 9 + D are not ready to groom and the number of debility cases to be evacuated is large. The appearance of the animals in 30 Brigade is much improved by the addition of a large number of remounts. Owing to the present as yet are remounts have had to be left unwatered this would not not need to be unhappy. This is particularly noticeable in D Battery 30 Brigade. Condition. This is particularly noticeable in D Battery 30 Brigade.	63/16
"	28/10/18		Visited and inspected the animals in the following units. No. 525 Company A.S.C. 9 th Durham Pioneer Battalion, 459 460 461 Companies R.E. & Signal Company 310 Brigade R.F.A. 185 & 187 Infantry	63/16
"	29/10/18		Inspected the animals of the following units. Brigades & M.G.	63/16
"	30/10/18		Visited and inspected the animals of the following units. 13 H. (O.R., MrGS., 152nd Infantry Brigade Machine Gun Battalion M. & H.Q. 250 Field Ambulance.	63/16
Houlemns	31/10/18		Moved from Bovillers to Houlemns. Th. M.V.S. to 65 moved from Treux Farm to Verbus Farm. Div C & T. Sect 54 (B). Inspected the animals of 3 + 6 Brigades R.F.A. 361 Section D.A.C and Signal Company.	63/16

C.E. Hall A/Capt A.V.C.
D.A.D.V.S. 63rd (N.R.) Division

(A7092). Wt. W12859/M1293. 75,000. 1/17. D. D. & L., Ltd. Forms/C.2118/14.

Original

Vol 24

Confidential
War Diary
H. A. R. V. S.
62nd (w.R) Divn

From 1~11~18   To 30~11~18

Volume XXIII

Army Form C. 2118.

WAR DIARY
or
INTELLIGENCE SUMMARY.
(Erase heading not required.)

Original

D.A.D.V.S. 62nd (2nd) Division

Instructions regarding War Diaries and Intelligence Summaries are contained in F. S. Regs., Part II. and the Staff Manual respectively. Title pages will be prepared in manuscript.

Place	Date	Hour	Summary of Events and Information	Remarks and references to Appendices
Péronne	1/11/18		Visits and inspects the animals in the following units Bde. M(R), M.O.R), Mr U.S. 457 & 460 R 461 st Companies R.E., No 2 & 3 Section D.A.C., & 8th Durham Rifles	57%
"	2/11/18		Attended Conference at D.A.D.S. Office D. Boyes. Inspects the 7/10 R.D. Mules and the animals of 458 Company R.E.	68%
"	3/11/18		Visits Mobile Vet. Section for M.O. to call & serves from Veterinary Farms 3 Pontus Proctor reports sick for M.O. to arrange from the following and My the 2 1/11th Infantry Bde. Reports by inspecting the animals of the following and My the 2 1/11th Infantry Bde. R.3rd Captain Mowton has broken 8 section V. detail sig. & hospital by Command. Veterinary Surgeon.	68%
Beaumont	4/11/18		Inspects the Mule of Brigade Vet. L.S. M(R) Mobile Surgeon Veterinary Hospital. Inspects the Mounts & Section D.A.C. reports sufficient at Beaumont. Inspects the animals 7/1 & Section R.E. T.	68%
"	5/11/18		Mr U.S., 459 & 461 Companies R.E. Inspects the Field Ambulance 459 & 461 Companies R.E. Visits the M(R), M.U.S. Selected a site for moves from Beauvain to Francy. Visits the M(R), M.U.S. Selected a site for M(R), 5th W & at Oursmel. Still there having on the move was unable to make inspection.	58%
Francy	6/11/18		M(R) Mobile Veterinary Section horses from Peronne to Oursmel Visits Peronne and inspects Showri Left Schwalimente to hand by 310th Brigade R.F.A. made army survey to collect and inspect animals of 156 & 157, 158 th Company a.s.c. Visits the following and 166 Infantry Brigade, 3/1st Brigade R.F.A. 185 Infantry Bde.	68%
"	7/11/18		457 & 460 Company R.E. all the mule are constantly on the move refer Kirchen remarks to carry out a satisfactory inspection of their animals. W(R), M.C.S. move from Oursmel to Vormigries.	68%
L Fredon	8/11/18		" from Vormigries to Le Fredon	68%
"	9/11/18		Inspects the animals of 185th Infantry Brigade. W(R) Field Ambulance, Nº 175 sections D.A.C. moves from Vormigries to Le Fredon	68%

WAR DIARY
of
INTELLIGENCE SUMMARY.

(Erase heading not required.)

D.A.D.V.S. 62 (WR) Division

Army Form C. 2118.

Place	Date	Hour	Summary of Events and Information	Remarks and references to Appendices
Hartcourt	10/11/18		Moved from C. Genolen to Hartcourt. Visits H(HR) M.V.S. Inspects the animals of 197, H(HR) Field Ambulance & 558 Company A.S.C. Capt Bryan A.V.C. returns from leave.	M.O.
Jonc le Bois	11/11/18		Moves from Hartcourt to Jonc le Bois. Casualties sustained at 11 oc today. Visits & inspects the animals of the following units. 1/5, 186th & 187th Infantry Brigades. 467 & 468 M.O. 's, Companies R.E., 5/3rd R.A.O. H.(HR) M.V.S. Proceeds from L. Genolen to Rest Camp. Capt. Brown proceeds to A.V.S. at	58/2
"	12/11/18		Gave charge during Capt. Cratt's absence on leave. Visits and inspects the animals on the following Units. H(HR) M.V.S. 310th Brigade R.F.A. No 1, 2 & 3 Sections D.A.C. 535 & 528 Company A.S.C. Capt Cratt goes on leave.	58/2
"	13/11/18		Inspects the animals of the following units. 312 H Brigade R.F.A. & (HR) M.V.S. B.T. 1/10 London Regiment, 1/5 Devons.	58/2
"	14/11/18		Held a conference of Veterinary Officers. Visits H(HR) M.V.S. Inspects the animals of the following units. Signal Company. M.V.S.P. 187th Wenley Brigade. Howe B Field Ambulance.	58/2
"	15/11/18		Visits A.D.V.S. L. Goy. & discusses arrangements as to evacuations & line of march. Inspects the animals of J. O.C. & D Companies, Machine Gun Battalion, 9th Dorset Pioneers, 8th Devons, and H(HR) MV.S.	58/2
"	16/11/18		Battery of Artillery being lame as to four of the two supplies animals on their route. Visit to B.H.S. Capt Williams A.V.C. T.O 1/C of A/t man A Brigade becomes part of the Division. Capt Williams A.V.C. T.O 1/C of last man Brigade inspects the animals of 558 Company A.S.C & the animals of the cyclists of this officer. Inspects animals on these routes. The am.	58/2
"	17/11/18		Visits & inspects the animals of the following units. 1/5, 62nd Infantry Bde. Signal Company. 2/1/6RVF M.V.S.	58/2

(A7092) WL W12890/M1793 75 10/60 1/17. D. D. & L., Ltd. Forms/C2118/14.

Army Form C. 2118.

WAR DIARY
of
INTELLIGENCE SUMMARY.
(Erase heading not required.)

D.A.D.V.S. 62nd (2nd) Division

Instructions regarding War Diaries and Intelligence Summaries are contained in F. S. Regs., Part II. and the Staff Manual respectively. Title pages will be prepared in manuscript.

Place	Date	Hour	Summary of Events and Information	Remarks and references to Appendices
Ham sur Heure	18/11/18		Moved from Bomal Bois to Ham-sur-Heure on the first stage of our journey to the Rhine	6876
"	19/11/18		H(QR) M.V.S. moved from Jemy-Heard to Pomezee.	6876
			Visited and inspected the animals of the following units. Vy. Machine Gun Battalion.	
			H(QR) Field Ambulance, 461st & 457th Companies R.E. 8th West Yorks & 13th Durham	6876
"	20/11/18		Inspected the animals of the following units – Vy. 14th Brigade R.H.A. 187th Infantry	
			Brigade. H(QR) M.V.S. moved from Pomezee to Cour-sur-Heure	6876
Cour-sur-Heure	21/11/18		Moved from Ham-Sur-Heure to Cour-sur-Heure. Visited H(QR) M.V.S. Inspected the animals	6876
			of 14th R.H.A., B.A.C. 186th Infantry Brigade, & 538 Company A.S.C.	
"	22/11/18		Inspected the animals of the following Units – Divisional Signal Company, 187th	6876
			Infantry Brigade, 25th Company H.C.C.	
"	23/11/18		Attended Conference at A.D.V.S. Office Charleroi. Inspected animals of 185th Infantry	6876
			Brigade.	6876
"	24/11/18		Inspected the animals of 187th Infantry Brigade 528th Company A.S.C.	6876
"	25/11/18		Moved from Cour-sur-Heure to Biesme. H(QR) M.V.S. arrived at Mareuil. Inspected	6876
			14th Brigade Ammunition Column animals.	
Biesme	26/11/18		Inspected the animals of the following Units. H(QR) M.V.S. Nos. 1 & 3 Sections	6876
			DAC. 186th Infantry Brigade & 555th Company A.S.C.	
"	27/11/18		Moved from Biesme to Leignon. The H(QR) M.V.S. moved from Mareuil to	
			Leignon. Inspected the animals of the following units – Vy 14th Brigade R.H.A. 556 Company	6876
			A.S.C. 185th Infantry Brigade Signal Company.	
"	28/11/18		Visited the following units – 62nd Machine Gun Battalion H(QR) Field Ambulance	
			457th & 461st Companies A.S.C. 9th Durham Pioneers. Animals generally showing the long	6876
			journeys, the animals of the Division are taking in condition	

Army Form C. 2113.

WAR DIARY
or
INTELLIGENCE SUMMARY.
(Erase heading not required.)

D.D.M.S. 62nd Division

Place	Date	Hour	Summary of Events and Information	Remarks and references to Appendices
Peyronne	29/9/18		Visited M.D.S. & to R of Peyronne. Inspected the arrivals for the following units: 310 Brigade the R.F.A. 2/3 Field Ambulance. of 2/1 Battalion March of the arrivals are hair twenty their condition fairly well, those of a fatigue sort are not looking well & as not regular. No movement. There have been no regular supply of forage for two or three days & not so long as the conditions exist it can only be expected the arrivals will show the strain.	658
	30/9/18		Inspected the arrivals 184 & 185 K.O.Y.L.I. Battalions. Investigated a reports outrages of YPS Ford Motor lorries to the Major of Sorel. To discuss search on the Field Ambulance Hdqrs. Gillemont Farm others in last look, Hams & dressings of Kurs on of Sorel. Drive Gourette thence billets Sorel & Haviour no losses until D.G.? sent all this hearing at front end of town to British troops. Visited the A.D.M.S. 16 Corps at Bienvent.	658

D.D.M.S. D.A.D.M.S. RASC
2nd. D.A.D. 62nd A.D. Division

Original

Confidential
War Diary
of
A.A.A. 63rd (unt) Div

Vol. XXIV

From 1-12-18   To 31-12-18

Original

Army Form C. 2118.

WAR DIARY
INTELLIGENCE SUMMARY.
(Erase heading not required.)

of D.A.D.V.S. 62nd (2nd R.) Division

Instructions regarding War Diaries and Intelligence Summaries are contained in F. S. Regs., Part II. and the Staff Manual respectively. Title pages will be prepared in manuscript.

Place	Date	Hour	Summary of Events and Information	Remarks and references to Appendices
Leignon	1/12/18		Visited and inspected the animals of 185th Infantry Brigade & 556th Company A.S.C also 2/(2R) Field Ambulance.	62R
"	2/12/18		Visited and inspected the animals of 1/4th R.H.A. Brigade & B.A.C.	65R
"	3/12/18		Inspected the animals of 186th Infantry Brigade	65R
"	4/12/18		Visited and inspected the animals of the following units:- V/y, 460, 461 & 457 Companies R.E. and 2/1 Durham Pioneer Battalion.	65R
"	5/12/18		Held a conference of V.O.s headed the animals of 62nd Divisional Mounted Gun. Battalion. Visited 2/(2R) M.V.S.	65R
"	6/12/18		Inspected the animals of 187th Infantry Brigade.	65R
"	7/12/18		Inspection of mares for breeding purposes, in accordance with instructions received from 9th Corps.	65R
"	8/12/18		Visited the A.D.V.S. 9 Corps at Denneel. Inspected Horses M.V.S. Headquarters 185th & 186th	65R
"	9/12/18		Visited inspected the animals of the following units:- R.A. Visits 31(2R) M.V.S.	65R
"	10/12/18		187th Infantry Brigade, and R.A. 2/1 Section D.A.C. A & C Batteries 310th Brigade R.F.A. & N° 1 Section D.A.C. Inspected the animals of 310th Brigade R.F.A. & N° 1 Section D.A.C.	65R
"	11/12/18		305 Bde animals are still in a bad condition & have improved little or none since the move. The M.O.R. M.V.S. moved from Thynes to Leignon	65R
"			2/1 (2R) moved to Remond Farm (map ref C.3.9.7.)	65R
"	12/1/19		March (Seed) from Leignon. Inspected the animals of 186th Infantry Brigade. 3/(2R) Field Ambulance. 3/(2R) Field Ambulance, 537 Company A.S.C	65R
"	13/1/19		Inspected the animals of the following units V/y, 187th Infantry Bde, 556th Company A.S.C. 75 (2R) (M.O.R.) M.V.S. moved from Remond Field Ambulance 3/10 & 313th Brigades R.F.A. & 2/(2R) M.V.S. Farm to Ville	65R

(A702) Wt W12530/M1293 75,000. 1/17. D. D. & L., Ltd. Forms/C.2118/14.

Original

Army Form C. 2118.

WAR DIARY
of
INTELLIGENCE SUMMARY.

(Erase heading not required.)

D.H.Q.S. 6." (MR) Division

Instructions regarding War Diaries and Intelligence Summaries are contained in F. S. Regs. Part II. and the Staff Manual respectively. Title pages will be prepared in manuscript.

Place	Date	Hour	Summary of Events and Information	Remarks and references to Appendices
Victoria	14/9/18		Moved from Legnano to Victoria. 7/(60R) M.G. moved from Ville to Rabies. Inspected the animals of No's 1, 2 & 3 sections D.H.C.	687%
"	15/9/18		Inspected the animals of 528 Company A.S.C. and reported to Headquarters D. on the low condition of some of the attached mules in this unit. Tactics inspected some animals of the 73 (MR) Field Ambulance, reported unable to travel.	687%
"	16/9/18		Moved from Victoria to Verona Cov.	687%
Montecchio	17/9/18		Moved from Verona to Montecchio. 7/(60R) M.G. moved from Grand Cov to Werona. Inspected the animals of the following units on the March, 63 310 & Brigade R.F.A. 525 & 528 Company A.S.C. 7/3 (60R) Field Ambulance sections D.H.Q. and 7/(60R) M.G.	687%
"	18/9/18		Had a conference of V.O's. Inspected animals of Divisional Head Quarters, Signal Company, 7/(60R) M.G.	687%
"	19/9/18		Inspected the animals of 3rd & Bde R.F.A. & 310 Bde R.F.A. Victor, 7/(60R) M.G.	687%
"	20/10/18		All ranks on the move unable to make inspection. 7/(60R) Moved from Werona to Eleonora Camp	687%
"	21/10/18		Moved from mercury to Kaltenleiten. 7/(60R) Moved from Eleonora Camp to Kaltenleiten. Inspected animals of Medium Gun Battalion, 184 Infantry Brigade, 528 Company A.S.C. & 7/(60R) Field Ambulance.	687%
Kaltenleiten	22/10/18			687%
"	23/10/18		Inspected the animals of 71 in R Brigade R.H.Q. 7/(60R) M.G. moved from Kaltenleiten to Kaltenkeren	687%

Army Form C. 2118.

WAR DIARY
of
INTELLIGENCE SUMMARY.
(Erase heading not required.)

D.D.M.S. 62nd (2/nd) Division.

Place	Date	Hour	Summary of Events and Information	Remarks and references to Appendices
Folkestone	24/1/18		Inspected animals of Nº C Battery 311th Brigade R.F.A. M.M.P. Divisional Head Quarters and Signal Company	65/18
"	25/1/18		Christmas day	
"			2/15R. Motor moved from Hortatr to Keldernish. Visited the A.D.V.S. & born at Everingham	6F/18 66/18
"	26/1/18		Inspected the animals of 525 Company L.S.C. Held a conference of V.O's	66/18
"	27/1/18		Visited & inspected the animals of the following units e.g. 1/4th & 1/5th Hampshire Battalions, 457 Company R.E. & 4th Field Coy, 2/6 Verona, S.A.O.C. L.S. attended in a tempt for the selection of brood mares in Horse Brigade of Artillery, D.I.V.S. any B.A.C.	69/18
"	28/1/18		Visited and inspected the animals of the following units by 186th Infantry Brigade 467 Company R.E. 62nd Machine Gun Battalion & 2/(2/2) Infantry Testis and inspected the animals of 311th Brigade R.F.A.	68/18 67/18
"	29/1/18		Visited 311th Brigade accompanied by the O.C. reports the animals of "D" Battery. Points out the bad condition of the fit & stewing of D Battery	68/18
"	30/1/18		The evening in both units in inspection of veterinary "D" Battery Inspected the animals of /4 "D" Battalion 186th Brigade R.I.A	68/18

O'Neill Major R.A.V.C.
A.D.V.S. 62nd (2/nd) Division.

19
Original

Confidential
War Diary
of
R.A.F., V.S.
63rd (Aux) Sqn.
From 1-1-19 to 31-1-19
Volume XXV

M 26

WAR DIARY of INTELLIGENCE SUMMARY

Army Form C. 2118.

Place	Date	Hour	Summary of Events and Information	Remarks and references to Appendices
Tollincourt	1/1/19		E.A.D.V.S. 63rd M.D. Division. Visited and inspected the animals of the following units. Viz: 84th and 104th Coys. R.E., 5th K.A.Y.R., the York Place, 84th Companies 2/1c Eucluian 46th & Company R.E. 1 animal was left at 4mbalation by the 111th Battery. The and 461st Company R.E. 1 animal was suffering from a skin wound & was put down in state, one mule to good general description, visited & talked to animal left behind by 111th Battery. The animal had been destroyed by order 4 from the A.D.V.S. due to the extent of laceration & lameness	6576
"	2/1/19		Held a suspected V.D. disease the animal belonging to the animals of 3rd Division. Visits and inspected the animals belonging to 16th Signal Company.	6576
"	3/1/19		Was accompanied by the O.C. 315th Brigade R.F.A. during my inspection of A & C batteries. Visited 21st H.A. A.A.	6576 6576
"	4/1/19		Attended conference at A.D.V.S. Office Eucluian.	6576
"	5/1/19		Veterinary Board consisting of Captain Crabb, Captain Shroud & Major E.E. Neill as President commenced the examination of animals as to soundness of the 315th Brigade. A & C batteries completed.	6576
"	6/1/19		The above board continued the examination of the animals of B & D batteries 315th Brigade and of battery 310th Brigade R.F.A. also Headquarters 315th Brigade R.F.A.	6576 6576
"	7/1/19		The Veterinary Board continued the examination of animals belonging to B, C & D Batteries & Headquarters 310th Brigade R.F.A.	6576
"	8/1/19		The above board with the exception of Capt. Shroud who was replaced by Captain Brown, Examined the animals of J, L, 400 & 401 Batteries 14th Brigade R.H.A.	6576

Army Form C. 2118.

Original WAR DIARY of INTELLIGENCE SUMMARY.

(Erase heading not required.)

D.A.D.V.S. 62nd (2nd WR) Division

Place	Date	Hour	Summary of Events and Information	Remarks and references to Appendices
Schleiden	9/1/19		Held a conference of V.O.s. Visited suspects animals on Divisional Head-Quarters	6911
"	10/1/19		Veterinary Board consisting of Major Hall (President) Captains Cratt & Brown continued the examination of the animals as 2 Commanders of No 1 Section D.A.C. & 4.2 Battery in Brigade R.H.A. & 147th Brigade Headquarters. The Board as above continued the examination of Nos 2 & 3 Sections and	6916
"	11/1/19		Headquarters D.A.C.	6916
"	12/1/19		The Board as constituted above continued the examination of the animals of the 114th Brigade R.F.A., B.A.C. Vanity & (60th) M.C.S.	6911
"	13/1/19		The Board above named examined the animals of 186th Infantry Brigade & 457th Company R.E.	6911
"	14/1/19		The Board as above examined animals of Signal Company & Divisional Head Quarters	6911
"	15/1/19		The Board as above examined the animals of the Machine Gun Battalion	6911
"	16/1/19		The Board examined the animals of 557 Company A.S.C. & 75 Fields Ambulance & 6911	6911
"	17/1/19		The Board examined the animals of 185th Infantry Brigade & 1/408 Field Ambulance	6911
"	18/1/19		Visited 3/1 (W.R.) M.T.S. suspects animals in Gleen D.& D. The Veterinary Board consisting of Major Hall President, Captains Strong and Cratt R.A.V.C. continued the examination of the animals of	6911
"	19/1/19		515 Company A.S.C., 466 T Company A.S.C. & 526 Y Company A.S.C.	6911

WAR DIARY of INTELLIGENCE SUMMARY

Army Form C. 2118.

Original

(Erase heading not required.)

D.A.D.V.S. 62nd (W.R.) Division

Place	Date	Hour	Summary of Events and Information	Remarks and references to Appendices
Villedieu	20/1/19		The Veterinary Board consisting of Major Neill (President), Captain Crabtt, Captain Bryan examined & classified the animals of the following units, Headquarters 187 Infantry Brigade, H.Q. and 3rd K.O.Y.L.I. & 6/13 Field Ambulance.	6576
"	21/1/19		The Board was about to confirm the examination & classification of the animals of the following units, 336 Company A.S.C. 461st Company A.S.C., 6/L, 7/L & 9th Durham Pioneers.	6876
"	22/1/19		The Veterinary Board consisting of Major Neill (President), Captain Crabtt & Captain Bryan entered the examination & classification of the animals in Headquarters Divisional Artillery & Headquarters R.E. Held a conference of Veterinary Officers & discussed the new classification of animals in relation to A.G. & arms & meetings.	6876
"	23/1/19			6876
"	24/1/19		Ordinary routine duties.	6876
"	25/1/19		Visited the A.D.V.S. IX Corps with reference to new average returns.	6876
"	26/1/19		Inspected the animals of Divisional Headquarters and Signal Company	6876
"	27/1/19		Visited & inspected the animals of 2/1st (W.R.) Field Ambulance, 9th Durham Pioneers, 1st York & Lancs & 336 Company A.S.C. & 1/1(W.R.) M.G.S.	6576
"	28/1/19		Owing to frost was unable to make inspection it being too dangerous to use as no cars available.	6576
"	29/1/19 30/1/19 31/1/19		Ordinary routine duties. Held a conference of Veterinary Officers. Inspected the animals of A & D Battery 310 Bdr. Field inspected the animals of B, C & D Battery 315 Brigade R.F.A.	6876 6876 6876

E.G.Neill Major R.A.V.C.
A.D.V.S. 62nd Division

Instructions regarding War Diaries and Intelligence Summaries are contained in F. S. Regs., Part II. and the Staff Manual respectively. Title pages will be prepared in manuscript.

WAR DIARY
or
INTELLIGENCE SUMMARY.
(Erase heading not required.)

Army Form C. 2118.

OFFICER I/C CHARGE RECORDS
-9 APR 1919
ROYAL ARMY VETY. CORPS.

Place	Date	Hour	Summary of Events and Information	Remarks and references to Appendices
Schladen	1/1/19		Visited and inspected the animals of the following units by 8th West Yorks, 1/5 Devons, 2/20 Londons, 460th Company R.E., 5th K.O.Y.L.I., 1/4 South Lancs, 508 Company A.S.C. and 461st Company R.E. 1 inspected horse left at Wollenstein by the 11th Battery. This animal was in a state of exhaustion, had suffered from a kick made off [illegible] got down in stable & was unable to rise. Ordered destruction. Visited Schmidt [illegible] examine animal left behind by 11th Battery, the animal had been destroyed by orders of some officer.	[initials]
"	2/1/19		Held a conference of V.O's discussed the subject of examination as to soundness of the animals of the Division. Visited and inspected the animals belonging to Signal Company.	[initials]
"	3/1/19		Was accompanied by the O.C. 312th Brigade R.F.A. during my inspection of A & C batteries. Visited 2/4 [illegible]	[initials]
"	4/1/19		Attended conference at A.D.V.S. Office Eickershen. Visited 2/[illegible]	[initials]
"	5/1/19		Veterinary Board consisting of Captain Crabb, Captain Strond & Major C.E. Neill as President commenced the examination of animals as to soundness of the 312th Brigade. A & C batteries completed.	[initials]
"	6/1/19		The above board continued the examination of the animals of B & D batteries 312th Brigade and a battery 310th Brigade R.F.A. also Headquarters 312th	[initials]
"	7/1/19		The Veterinary Board continued the examination of animals belonging to B, C & D Batteries & Headquarters 310th Brigade R.F.A.	
"	8/1/19		The above board with the exception of Capt. Strond who was replaced by Capt. [illegible] examined the animals of [illegible] 400 & 401 Batteries 12th Brigade R.H.A.	[initials]

(A7092) Wt. W12839/M1293. 750,000. 1/17. D. D. & L., Ltd. Forms/C.2118/14.

WAR DIARY or INTELLIGENCE SUMMARY

Army Form C. 2118.

Place	Date	Hour	Summary of Events and Information	Remarks and references to Appendices
Rotterdam	9/1/19		Held a conference of T.O. regarding reports awaited re Remounts etc. Question.	
"	10/1/19		Returning Board consisting of Major Hall (President), Captain Buxter-Brown, visited the remounts, 1 officer, 1 N.C.O. and sick of 1st Section R.A.V.C. & 2 Batts. 3 Infantry Bde + 11 & 21 gds. Recognized the horses as above listed and the men as above. 7 officers, 3 horses and headquarters BAC.	
"	11/1/19			
"	12/1/19		The board re-constituted above continued the examination of the remounts of the 1st Brigade R.F.A., B.H.Q. Vet Off 61 (drs) R.E.S.	
"	13/1/19		The above named examined the remounts of 186th Infantry Brigade + 457th Company R.E.	
"	14/1/19		The board as above examined remounts of Royal Company + Divisional H.Q. Grouters.	
"	15/1/19		The Board as above examined the remounts of the Hussars 6th Battalion Company A.S.C. & 31 Field Ambulance.	
"	16/1/19		The Board examined the remounts of 115th Infantry Brigade + H.Q. + held	
"	7/1/19		continue.	
"	8/1/19		Visited 3/1 (HLFI) in M.T. transports camped in Class D + D.	
"	9/1/19		The Veterinary Board consisting of Major Hall President, Captain Xmas and Craig R.A.V.C. continued the re-inspection of the animals of 313 Company A.S.C., 460 Company R.E. + 312 Company A.S.C.	

Army Form C. 2118.

WAR DIARY
of
INTELLIGENCE SUMMARY.
(Erase heading not required.)

Instructions regarding War Diaries and Intelligence Summaries are contained in F. S. Regs., Part II. and the Staff Manual respectively. Title pages will be prepared in manuscript.

Place	Date	Hour	Summary of Events and Information	Remarks and references to Appendices
Salonica	20/4/19		The Veterinary Board consisting of Major Held (President) Captain Byrne examined & classified the animals of the following units: Headquarters 19th Infantry Brigade, the mens of 2nd K.O.Y.L.I. & D/3 Field Ambulance.	Oct.
	21/4/19		H.Q. Sunshade Capt. examined the majority of the 1st R.A. animals of the following units & Coy & 3/6 ten of Company F.S.C., C/10, Y.J. & G.F. Buchan Butter.	Oct.
	22/4/19		The Veterinary Board continuing of Major Held (President) Captain Evens & Butler continued the examination & classification of the animals Headquarters Division Artillery, Headquarters F.A. Veterinary Officers, attended to new classification of animals and the probation of & of Horses & Battery.	Oct.
	23/4/19		Ordinary routine duties	Oct.
	24/4/19		Visit the H.Q. & S.A.A. Corps and reported to run avenge return respects the arrival of Division Headquarters and signal Company	Oct.
	25/4/19		Visit respects the animals of Returns Field Ambulance, F.F. Buchan Butter.	Oct.
	26/4/19		Return the Pack Horses & S.F. Company A.S.C. & MOD. & G. Only 1 horse was made to now inspection & having to depart horse in our day available.	Oct.
	27/4/19		Ordinary routine duties.	Oct.
	28/4/19 30/4/19		Had a conference of Veterinary Officers. Subjects arranged: H.D. Return mobile H./F.3.	Oct.
	31/4/19			Oct.

E. F. Hall A/Capt. R.A.V.C. ADVS. 62nd. D.

Original

16 W24

Confidential

War Diary
of
D.A.D.V.S. 23rd (NZ) Divn

From 1-2-19   To 28-2-19

Vol XXVI

Original

Army Form C. 2118.

WAR DIARY
INTELLIGENCE SUMMARY.
(Erase heading not required.)

MAJ. 64th(4th) Division

Instructions regarding War Diaries and Intelligence Summaries are contained in F. S. Regs., Part II. and the Staff Manual respectively. Title pages will be prepared in manuscript.

Place	Date	Hour	Summary of Events and Information	Remarks and references to Appendices
Schleiden	1/2/19		Visited and inspected the animals in the following Units. Hq. Nos. 1, 2 & 3 Sections D.A.C. 4th Brigade B.A.C. and 7/1 (4th) Bn. M.G.S.	CRN
"	2/2/19		Routine duties	CRN
"	3/2/19		Visited and inspected the animals B & C Batteries 310th Brigade R.F.A. and 73rd & 4 Battery 313 th Brigade R.F.A.	CRN
"	4/2/19		Visited and inspected the animals of J & 400 Batteries 14th Brigade R.H.A.	CRN
"	5/2/19		Inspected the animals of C Battery 313 th Brigade R.F.A. and 535 Company A.S.C.	CRN
"	6/2/19		Offer a Conference of P.O. Visited and inspected the animals of 180th Brigade 74, 75, 76 & 538 Company A.S.C. also 461 Company R.E.	CRN
"	7/2/19		Inspected animals purchased by Civilians from Germany Army during the retreat. 40 were collected by 189th Bde & 1 by 186 Bde. Many of these animals were hungry and are a great source of danger to British animals billeted in the same village. Inspected the animals of 2/3 R.F. Field Ambulance	CRN
"	8/2/19		Visited H(4th) M.T.C. Inspected animals in No 2 & 3 Sections D.A.C.	CRN
"	9/2/19		Visited D Battery 313 th Brigade. Inspected animals Divisional Headquarters	CRN
"	10/2/19		Accompanied the A.D.V.S. on his inspection of H(4th) M.T.C. he also inspected the animals in 400, 401 Batteries 14th Brigade R.H.A. D Battery 313th Brigade R.F.A. and C Battery 315th Bde. R.F.A.	CRN
"	11/2/19		Inspected the animals in J Battery 14 Bde. Headquarters & B & D Batteries 314th Brigade R.F.A.	CRN

Army Form C. 2118.

WAR DIARY
of
INTELLIGENCE SUMMARY.

(Erase heading not required.)

2nd/5th 62nd (W.R.) Division   Original

Instructions regarding War Diaries and Intelligence Summaries are contained in F. S. Regs., Part II. and the Staff Manual respectively. Title pages will be prepared in manuscript.

Place	Date	Hour	Summary of Events and Information	Remarks and references to Appendices
Schliden	12/2/19		Inspected animals of Divisional Headquarters & Signal Company.	D.R.E
"	13/2/19		Took over duties of A.D.V.S. from Major Hall R.A.V.C. Received A.F.s A. 2000 Stow V.Os and F.S. animals in No 3 Section D.A.C. also in No 1 Station S.A.C.	D.P.S.
"	14/2/19		Inspected animals Y and Z in No 62nd D.A.C. and in 62nd Div Signal Coy.	D.P.S.
"	15/2/19		Inspected animal mallened in D.H.Q. and in Signal Coy. Also mallened animals in No 1 Section and H.Q of D.A.C.	D.P.S.
"	16/2/19			D.R.E.
"	17/2/19		Inspected animals mallened in No 1 Sect and H.Q D.A.C. also inspected animals in 4th B.A.C. and visited H.Q (W.R) M.V.S.	D.P.S.
"	18/2/19		Inspected animals in 7th, 310 Bde and Captain Street.	D.R.E.
"	19/2/19		Visited H.Q (W.R) M.V.S and examined animals in No 3 Section D.A.C	D.P.S.
"	20/2/19		Received A.F.s A 2001 from V.O's and examined animals in No 3 Section D.A.C.	D.P.S.
"	21/2/19		Visited H.Q (W.R) M.V.S, and examined animals for casting as Z.Ds.	D.P.S.
"	"		Mallened animals in No 2 Section D.A.C.	D.R.E.
"	22/2/19		Examined Animals in 312 Bde with Capt Street, Examined animals in 2 DAC	D.R.E.
"	23/2/19		Visited 2/1 (W.R) M.V.S. and examined animals in 4th B.A.C.	D.R.E.
"	24/2/19		Visited and examined animals in D.H.Q and Signal Coy	D.R.E.
"	25/2/19		Visited animals in M.V.S and inspected animals in 310 Bde R.F.A with Capt Stow	D.R.E.
"	26/2/19		Inspected animals in 4th Bde R.H.A. for Z.D classification	D.R.E.

Army Form C. 2118.

WAR DIARY
or
INTELLIGENCE SUMMARY.

Original

(Erase heading not required.) D.A.D.V.S. 62nd Division

Instructions regarding War Diaries and Intelligence Summaries are contained in F. S. Regs., Part II. and the Staff Manual respectively. Title pages will be prepared in manuscript.

Place	Date	Hour	Summary of Events and Information	Remarks and references to Appendices
Schilden	24.2.18		Inspected German civilian horses for refunds in 186th and 187th Bde areas	DKL
	26.2.18		Visited 310 and 312 Bdes R.F.A. with Captain Stead and Mallinson	
			amounts in 525 Cuy A.L.E.	DKL

D.R. Gibb
Capt. R.A.V.C.
A/D.A.D.V.S.
62nd Division

Army Form C. 2118.

OFFICER-IN-
[stamp] -9 APR 1919
ROYAL ARMY VETY. CORPS

WAR DIARY
or
INTELLIGENCE SUMMARY.
(Erase heading not required.)

Instructions regarding War Diaries and Intelligence Summaries are contained in F.S. Regs., Part II. and the Staff Manual respectively. Title pages will be prepared in manuscript.

D.H.M.S. 62nd (2nd West Lancs) Division

Place	Date	Hour	Summary of Events and Information	Remarks and references to Appendices
St Andre	1/2/19		Visited and inspected the animals in the Lines of Units Hy, Hd 1 & 2, H.T. Sections Hy, 4th Brigade.	/FN
"	2/2/19		4th Brigade. B, D & E and 21 (MM) Bdr. R.A. Routine office work	/FN
"	3/2/19		Visited and inspected B & C Batteries 310th Brigade R.H.A. and Br. H. Battery 310 & H. Brigade R.H.A.	/FN /FN /FN
"	4/2/19		Visited and inspected the animals of Y & Z.00 Batteries 14th Brigade R.H.A.	/FN
"	5/2/19		Inspected the animals of E Battery 313th Brigade R.H.A. and 331st Company A.S.C.	/FN
"	6/2/19		Was a journey of 6 B Visits and inspected the animals of 183 R Brigade. Y 4 Y J & 538 Company A.S.C. also 461 Company R.E.	/FN
"	7/2/19		Inspected animal purchases by Civilians from Germans Army during the retreat. 45 were collected by 184 & 185 Bde & 184 & 186 Bde. Army of the Rhine and having one a great source of danger to British and British in the same thing. Inspected the attitudes of 98 MRL Field Ambulance D.A.C.	/FN
"	8/2/19		Visited 7th MRI, M.615 and 33th Brigade, inspected animals in 9th & 3rd sections D.A.C.	/FN
"	9/2/19		Visited D Battery 311 Brigade. Inspected animals in same thing.	/FN
"	10/2/19		Accompanied the A.D.V.S. on his inspection of 7 MRI, M.10 he also inspected the animals in M.0D, 201 Battery in Mezzepel, RHA. D Battery 311 Brigade one C Battery 319 Bde 146, inspected the animals in J Battery 14 Bde, Headquarters D.A.C. total Corps. 530	/FN

Battens. D. H. Cowper Lt Cl. |

Army Form C. 2118.

WAR DIARY
or
INTELLIGENCE SUMMARY.

(Erase heading not required.)

Instructions regarding War Diaries and Intelligence Summaries are contained in F.S. Regs., Part II. and the Staff Manual respectively. Title pages will be prepared in manuscript.

Place	Date	Hour	Summary of Events and Information	Remarks and references to Appendices
Salonica	17/2/19		Inspected animals of Divisional Headquarters & Signal Company.	
	18/2/19		Took over duties of A.D.V.S. from Major R.A.V.C. Bradshaw and reported M.O's [?]	
	19/2/19		fit for Benefit [?] on [?] 3/A.V.C. also [?] on [?] from D.A.C.	
	20/2/19		Visited animals Zone 2 of 62nd T.M.B. [?] & Divn Signal Coy	
	16/2/19		Inspected animals mentioned in D.H.Q. and Divl Signal Coy also [?] not seen [?]	
			animals not detached with Divl D.A.C.	
	17/2/19		Inspected animals mentioned in [?] last [?] and H.Q. D.A.C. also ambulance	
			wagons of 4th D.A.C. and visited of (M.R.) M.V.S.	
	18/2/19		Sent [?] [?] on 7th M.C.B. on [?] [?]	
	19/2/19		Visited of (M.R.) R.V.S. and inspected animals on 3 Inbox V.A.C.	
	20/2/19		Received N.P.T. A 200 from [?] T.O. and examined animals on the 3 Inbox D.A.C.	
	21/2/19		Visited of (M.R.) M.V.S. and examined animals of battery on Z.O.s	
	"		Walkover animals on Zs. of [?] D.A.C.	
	22/2/19		Examined horses on 228 Bde 20th Cyps Stragglers guards 2DAP	
	23/2/19		Visited of (M.R.) M.V.S. and examined animals on 4th B.A.C.	
	24/2/19		Visited and inspected animals of H.Q. and Signal Coy	
			[?]	
			Inspected [?] [?] of [?]	

Army Form C. 2118.

WAR DIARY
or
INTELLIGENCE SUMMARY.
(Erase heading not required.)

Instructions regarding War Diaries and Intelligence Summaries are contained in F. S. Regs., Part II. and the Staff Manual respectively. Title pages will be prepared in manuscript.

Place	Date	Hour	Summary of Events and Information	Remarks and references to Appendices

Confidential.

92

Original.

No 46 (2nd two)

War Diary
of
D.A.D.S. Highland Div.

From 1-3-19 To 31-3-19

Vol XXVII

Army Form C. 2118.

WAR DIARY
INTELLIGENCE SUMMARY.
(Erase heading not required.)

D.A.D.V.S. 62nd Division.

Place	Date	Hour	Summary of Events and Information	Remarks and references to Appendices
Solesmes	1-3-19		Visited 2/(W.R) M.V.S. and inspected animals for evacuation. Inspected also animals mentioned in 325 Coy A.S.C.	S.P.6
"	2-3-19		Inspected animals in D.H.Q.	S.P.6
"	3-3-19		Visited 2/(W.R) M.V.S. and accompanied A.D.V.S. W. Corps in his inspection of animals in 14th Bde R.H.A. and also inspected with him an outbreak of influenza in 4th B.A.C.	S.P.6
"	4-3-19		Inspected animals of Signal Coy 62nd Division also animals in 3rd Bde.	S.P.8.
"	4/3/19		Returned from leave & resumed duty. Undertook an outbreak of contagious influenza has taken place amongst the animals of the B.A.C. 1st Brigade R.H.A.	S.P.2
"	5/3/19		Visits respecting the animals of the B.A.C. in 1 Brigade R.H.A. Investigated the outbreak of influenza amongst the animals of this unit. Three animals have died from the disease (1 heavy draw & 2 mules) and at present there are 8 animals affected (7 h & 1 horse m. mules). The animals that have contracted the disease are all stabled in an old chicken shed, another section of animals belonging to same unit occupy a stable in the above mentioned shed but none of these have contracted the disease	S.P.L

Army Form C. 2118.

WAR DIARY
or
INTELLIGENCE SUMMARY

(Erase heading not required.)

D.A.D.V.S. 62nd W.R. Division

Place	Date	Hour	Summary of Events and Information	Remarks and references to Appendices
Achicourt	5/3/19		Symptoms of Disease. General depression. Capricious appetite. Temperature rarely little above tickler at beginning, but in the course of 12 to 24 hours, temp. may rise to 103° or even 105°. Pulse feeble & accelerated between 60 & 70 beats. Glands enlarged, nose and mouth lymphatic. Inanition and depression normal. Death usually sudden & unsuspected. Treatment Consists principally of good nursing. Hypodermic injections of Strychnine. Antiseptic inhalations. Discharge of Glands. R.E. Inspected the animals of Divisional Head quarters & 6/7 Horse batal Visited inspected the animals of the following units, 460 Company R.E.	697/1
"	6/3/19		1/5 Devons, 8 West Yorks & 326 Company H.B.C. Visited and inspected the animals in the B.A.C. in 4 Brigade. The Influenza cases are progressing fairly well except two horses. These two animals have a temperature of 104°, breathing rather distressed, in one of these animals it was thought advisable to perform Tracheotomy. Visited 2/COLR, R.F.	697/1
"	7/3/19		Inspected the animals. T.B. Battery 315th Brigade R.F.A. 315 Company H.T.C. Inspected the animals of D & C Batteries 30th Brigade R.F.A. Visited the B.A.C 4 Brigade, another horse affected with Influenza, died this morning & two others very ill & look like dying. Inspected Horses, m.t.s.	697/2
"	8/3/19			697/2
"	9/3/19		Inspected the animals of Divisional Signal Company.	697/2

Army Form C. 2118.

WAR DIARY
INTELLIGENCE SUMMARY.
(Erase heading not required.)

A.D.V.S. 62nd Division

Place	Date	Hour	Summary of Events and Information	Remarks and references to Appendices
Schieden	10/3/19		Vet's inspected the animals of the following units viz. Nos 1, 2, + 3 sections D.A.C. X Battery R.H.A. Brigades in Brigade R.H.A. Inspected the pithening cases in the B.A.C. in H. Brigade two horses died during the morning. There are still two mules very ill. Sanctioned evacuation to have the latter two animals destroyed. Sanctioned evacuation to the R.A.V.C. IX Corps to inform them of the action I was taking. The concerned. Inspected animals of Battery 313th Brigade R.F.A. Visited 3/169 M.O.S.	692 / 692
"	11/3/19		Vet's inspected the animals of the following units V/3 A & D Batteries 310th Brigade R.F.A., B, C, + D Battery 315th Brigade R.F.A.	692 / 692
"	12/3/19		Head Office routine. Unable to make any inspection as no cars available today.	
Duren	13/3/19		Have proceeded to new area on this date. Proceeded from Schieden to Duren.	692 / 692
"	14/3/19		Vet's acted locatio around Duren to select site for 2/(169) A.V.S. Inspected the animals of Divisional Machine Gun Battalion, 358 Company R.A.S.C.	692
"	15/3/19		Visited the following units respecting the animals 1/5 Royal Highlanders, 1/(60R) Field Ambulance, 466 Company R.E. Headquarters 187th Infantry Brigade.	692
"	16/3/19		Visited Inspected & met A.D.V.S. VI Corps	692
"	17/3/19		Vet's inspected the influenza cases at Kellwerich, one mule destroyed on the 16th inst. Advised Thos Morming there still remains under suspicion 3 mules + about — horses. Visited 2/(60R) M.V.S.	692
"	18/3/19		Vet's and inspected the animals of the following units: 1/5th Infantry Brigade - 1855th R.E. and 2/(169) Field Ambulance. 556 Company R.A.S.C, 466 Company R.E. West Yorks. 1/5 Devons 2/20 London's ant.	692
"	19/3/19		Inspected the animals in following units: 2/(60R) Field Ambulance, at	692

Army Form C. 2118.

WAR DIARY
INTELLIGENCE SUMMARY.
(Erase heading not required.)

of DADVS Highland Division

Place	Date	Hour	Summary of Events and Information	Remarks and references to Appendices
Divon	19/3/19		0/2 animals sent to Cologne for sale.	687/6
"	20/3/19		R.E. with the object of taking them over for this Division. Inspects the animals of Machine Gun Battalion & Divisional Signal Company.	687/6
"	21/3/19		Visits the Influenza cases at Tilmoush, all appear to be going on satisfactorily, and no fresh cases. Inspects the animals of "D", "E", "F", & 401 Batteries in R. Brigade R.H.A. "D" & "B" Batteries 317 R. Brigade and "G" Battery 316 R Brigade R.H.A.	687/6 687/6
"	22/3/19		Visited and inspected the animals on Headquarters 187 R. Infantry Brigade	687/6
"	23/3/19		A.D.V.S. II Corps called at this office accompanied him to aerodrome for 4 W.E.S.	687/6
"	24/3/19		Inspects the animals of the following units, 7hy Highland Machine Gun Battalion. Divisional Signal Company, and 558 Company R.A.S.C. The others were hollowed on 5th inst. Inspector greater in all.	687/6
"	25/3/19		Visits and inspects the animals in the following units. Fry the Seaforth Battalion. 7th Gordons. 5th Argyle Sutherlands Highlanders. 5th Gordons and 55 R Company R.A.S.C. The animals of the 1/4 Seaforths are a very inferior lot particularly the light draught team & one or two heavy draught. Several officers reported no cars available for inspection Jominals	687/6
"	26/3/19		Visits and inspects the animals of 526 Company R.A.S.C.	587/6
"	27/3/19		Inspects the animals of No 25 T.B.A.C. 11 R Brigade. R.H.A 40 Field Ambulance R.A.C.O Company R.E. 3(1000) No 25 T.B.A.C. 11 R Brigade. R.H.A	687/6 687/6
"	28/3/19		Inspects the animals of Divisional Headquarters. Lieut A Maclean R.A.C.O reports for duty	687/6
"	29/3/19		Attended conference at IV Corps Headquarters. Attended at IV Corps Headquarters in the afternoon was presented to Sir Douglas Haig Captain W.L. Darling reports for duty. Inspected animals on Divisional Headquarters	687/6 687/6
"	30/3/19			

Army Form C. 2118.

WAR DIARY
of
INTELLIGENCE SUMMARY.
(Erase heading not required.)

D.A.D.V.S. Highland Division

Instructions regarding War Diaries and Intelligence Summaries are contained in F. S. Regs., Part II. and the Staff Manual respectively. Title pages will be prepared in manuscript.

Place	Date	Hour	Summary of Events and Information	Remarks and references to Appendices
Duren	2/3/19		Tools & inspected the animals of 526 Company R.A.S.C. The B.A.C. 14th Brigade R.H.A. & 3/1VRS to V.S. Captain Darling posted temporarily to 125th Infantry Brigade	65/16
			O'Neill Major R.A.V.C. D.A.D.V.S. Highland Division	

Instructions regarding War Diaries and Intelligence Summaries are contained in F. S. Regs., Part II. and the Staff Manual respectively. Title pages will be prepared in manuscript.

WAR DIARY
or
INTELLIGENCE SUMMARY.
(Erase heading not required.)

Army Form C. 2118.

Place	Date	Hour	Summary of Events and Information	Remarks and references to Appendices
[illegible]	5/3/19		[illegible]	
"	6/3/19		[illegible] Inspected the animals of [illegible] Head Quarters & 6th Bn [illegible] [illegible] inspected the animals of the following units: 460 Company R.E. 1/3 Devons 8 West Yorks & 536th Company A.S.C.	[illegible]
	7/3/19		Visited and inspected the animals in the B.A.C. [illegible] Brigade. The following cases are progressing fairly well [illegible] [illegible]	[illegible]
	8/3/19		Inspected the animals of [illegible] Battery [illegible] Brigade R.F.A. & 536 Company A.S.C. Inspected the animals of [illegible] Battery [illegible] Brigade R.F.A. Visited the B.A.C. [illegible]	[illegible]
	9/3/19		Inspected the animals of [illegible]	

(A7092). Wt W12839/M1293 75,000. 1/17. D. D. & L., Ltd. Forms/C.2118/14.

WAR DIARY
or
INTELLIGENCE SUMMARY
(Erase heading not required)

Army Form C. 2118.

Place	Date	Hour	Summary of Events and Information	Remarks and references to Appendices
Sittingbourne	10/3/19		Visited & inspected the animals of the following units viz: No. 1, 2 & 3 sections R.G.C. & Battery in Brigade R.H.A. Inspected all hitherto cases in the R.G.C. in M. Brigade two were sick during the morning. The are still too much very ill. Arrangements to have the late two animals destroyed. Inspected the M.O.R.S. Horserails in Corps to inspect these of the actions. I was taking the Commercial.	67/2, 67/2
"	11/3/19		Inspected animals of A Battery, 315th Brigade R.H.A. Visited M.O.R.S. M.V.C. Visited & inspected the animals of the following units viz: A, C, & D Batteries 315 Brigade R.G.A., B, C, & D Bath. 315th Brig. T R.G.A.	67/2
"	12/3/19		Head Office matters: Unable to make any inspection as no cars available, transport provided to un-use on the date. Proceeded from Sittingbourne to Dover.	67/2, 67/2
Dover	13/3/19		Visited several localities around Dover & selected ists for 3/1(M.R.) M.V.S.	67/2
"	14/3/19		Inspected the animals of Divisional Signal Coys Battalion, 328 Company R.G.C.O.	67/2
"	15/3/19		Visited the following units: ½ Royal Hampshire, ¼(M.R.) Field Ambulance with 4th Company R.E. Bridgehead 187 Infantry Brigade. Visited, Incidentally & heat A.D.V.S. VI Corps	67/2, 67/2
"	16/3/19		Visited & inspected the Infantry Camps at Kildencot, animals selected on were developed in the 16th May 1918 this morning, there still remains under suspicion 3 mules & 1 horse. Tracks all dead in it.	67/2
"	18/3/19		Visited and inspected the animals of the following units: 185th Infantry Brigade, 556 Company R.A.S.C., 460 Company R.E. & ½ 1/1(M.R.) Field Ambulance, 8th West rode 13 Devons & ½ London's art, 1/ 1(M.R.) Field Ambulance.	67/2
"	19/3/19			67/2

WAR DIARY
INTELLIGENCE SUMMARY

Army Form C. 2118.

DADOS Highland Division

Place	Date	Hour	Summary of Events and Information	Remarks and references to Appendices
Duren	19/3/19		D/2 arrived and to Cologne for sale. Inspected the arrival of the 33rd Company R.E. with the object of taking them on for this Division.	887b
"	20/3/19		Inspected the animals of 9 machine Gun Battalion & Divisional Signal Company.	887b
"	21/3/19		Visited the influenza cases at Rheinard, all appear to be going on satisfactorily, and no fresh cases reported. The animals of T.T.F. & 401 Batteries 14 R Brigade R.H.A. D & B batteries & battery 110 R Brigade R.F.A.	887b
"	22/3/19		Visited and inspected the animals on Headquarters 186 R Infantry Brigade. 33 R Brigade and E battery 110 R Brigade R.F.A.	6.E.16
"	23/3/19		A.D.O.S. II Corps called re the three consignments now to start date Jan. 4 & 5 & 2 & 5. Inspected the animals of the following units. Sig. Highland machine Gun Battalion Divisional Signal Company & No. 558 Company R.A.S.C. The take were stabled on straw and together weather is cold.	887b
"	24/3/19		Visited and inspected the animals on the following units. By the Seaforth Battalion 1/4 Gordons 5th Argyle Sutherland Highlanders, 37 Locknow and 337 3rd Company R.A.S.C. The animals of the 1/4 Seaforths are a very inferior type animals the light draught horses are one or two heavy draught.	887b
"	25/3/19		Ordnance officer reporting no case exists.	887b
"	26/3/19		Visited and inspected the animals of 536 Company R.A.S.C. 14 R Brigade T.H.m 1 R.H.A 460 >11 Fires Co. Horses R.E. Field Co.	886b 887b
"	27/3/19		Inspected the animals on Divisional Headquarters. Kind n numbers R&6.0 reported for duty.	887b
"	28/3/19			887b
"	29/3/19		Started to prepare an II Corps Inspection. Arrived at II Corps on 7th afternoon.	888b
"	30/3/19		Was preceded by Lt. Douglas they kindly three or are in some of Inspection.	887b 886b

Army Form C. 2118.

WAR DIARY
of
INTELLIGENCE SUMMARY.
(Erase heading not required.)

D.A.D.S. Highland Division

Place	Date	Hour	Summary of Events and Information	Remarks and references to Appendices
Rouen	31/3/19		Today's inspected the animals of 536 Company R.A.S.C. The D.A.C. 14 Brigade R.F.A. & Captain Stanley proved temporarily to 103rd Infantry Brigade	6th

E.T. Wild Major R.A.V.C.
D.A.D.V.S. Highland Division

To
Officer i/c. R.A.V.C
Records. Woolwich.

D.A.D.V.S., DIVISION
No. V/406
Date. 8.5.19

Herewith Original War Diary
for the month April. 1919.

W.H. Austin
Capt. R.A.V.C
A/D.A.D.V.S
Highland Division.

Original

Confidential

War Diary

of

D.A.D.V.S.

Highland Division

From 1.4.19. To 30.4.19

Vol. XXVIII

Original

Army Form C. 2118.

WAR DIARY
of
INTELLIGENCE SUMMARY.
(Erase heading not required.)

Instructions regarding War Diaries and Intelligence Summaries are contained in F. S. Regs., Part II. and the Staff Manual respectively. Title pages ROYAL ARMY VETY. CORPS. will be prepared in manuscript.

D.A.D.V.S. Highland Division

Place	Date	Hour	Summary of Events and Information	Remarks and references to Appendices
Rouen	1/4/19		Inspected convoy to influenza. Lieut N. M. Crawford R.A.V.C. reports for duty	572
"	2/4/19		remounts temporarily to Mr I Brigade R.V.O. suffering from influenza, only fit to carry on office routine	572
"	3/4/19		do do do do	572
"	4/4/19		Capt W.A. Friston R.A.V.C. reports for duty, mane posted to 1/102 M.V.S. Inspected	572
"	5/4/19		the animals of 187 Infantry Brigade.	572
"	6/4/19		Inspected animals of Divisional Hdqrs Squadron, Signal Company & Machine Gun Battalion. Inspected 360 Z animals at troopfield Down prior to entraining for Base	572
"	7/4/19		Routine duties	572
"			"	
"	8-4-19		Took over duties of D.A.D.V.S. Highland Division	576
"	9-4-19		Inspected Horses in F.M.O. and Inspected horses at Brickfields available Camp	576
"	10-4-19		Routine Duties	576
"	11-4-19		Handed over duties of D.A.D.V.S. D.A.D.V.S. Capt Foster R.A.V.C.	576

N.M. Crawford
Major R.A.V.C.
D.A.D.V.S. Highland Division

J.R. Gabb
Capt. R.A.V.C.
A.D.V.S. Highland Div.

Army Form C. 2118.

WAR DIARY
or
INTELLIGENCE SUMMARY.
(Erase heading not required.)

Instructions regarding War Diaries and Intelligence Summaries are contained in F. S. Regs., Part II. and the Staff Manual respectively. Title pages will be prepared in manuscript.

Place	Date	Hour	Summary of Events and Information	Remarks and references to Appendices
Dures	12.4.19		Inspected animals at Concentration Camp Dueren, interviewed D.A.Q.M.G. Camp Commandant re arrangements to inspect animals on D.H.Q. following day. Inspected animals of H.Q. 1st F. Lot. Bde. accompany 2.30 p.m. accompanied M.D.C. & A.R.M. to inspect all animals on Div. H.Q.	A.D.V.S.
	13.4.19		Inspected animals at Concentration Camp Dueren + 1st & 2nd F.A. ambulances I.O.M. 1st F. Bgd. Bde., Bgd. Decoding Stations	A.D.V.S.
	14.4.19		Inspected animals at Concentration Camp Dueren, also 3 Coys animals of Div. H.Q. also A D.V.S.4 & 5 Corps, today M.V.S. Guards Div.	A.D.V.S.
	15.4.19		Inspected animals at Concentration Camp Dueren, 14 Lorries + 1 Pack transport sick to Mob.V.E.S. Animals inspected at Div. M.Q. Apel Horses charger + Peny of M.M.P. evacuated to Mob.V.E.S. Cairnels of 51st M.G.C. (Horses) inspected Visited 4 Mob. Bakery M.V.S.	A.D.V.S.
	17.4.19		Inspected animals at Concentration Camp Dueren. Visited A.D.V.S. IV Corps. Inspected animals at R.E. Signals Division, A1 animals & A.D. evacuated to 6.4 V.E.S.	A.D.V.S.
	18.4.19		Inspected animal at Concentration Camp Dueren + transferred 5 Horses + 1 mule to H.V.E.S. Visited M.G.C. Brickfields at Nora & 336 Lose with Colic - also at 6.30 p.m.	A.D.V.S.
	19.4.19		Visited M.G.C. Brickfields to make post mortem on horse which died previous day. Proceeded to T.E. Camp MONTZEN to identify mules taken by the Belgian Army, & arranged for it' departure to Concentration Camp Dueren following day.	A.D.V.S.
	20.4.19		Inspected Horses on Div. H.Q. Visited Horse Concentration Camp	A.D.V.S.
	21.4.19		Inspected Horses on Div.H.Q. Visited Concentration Camp Dueren - 6 Mules + 1 Horse evacuated to M.V.E.S.	A.D.V.S.

Original

Army Form C. 2118.

WAR DIARY or INTELLIGENCE SUMMARY.
(Erase heading not required.)

Army Vet. Corps. H.Q. D.A.D.V.S. Highland Division

Instructions regarding War Diaries and Intelligence Summaries are contained in F.S. Regs., Part II. and the Staff Manual respectively. Title pages will be prepared in manuscript.

Place	Date	Hour	Summary of Events and Information	Remarks and references to Appendices
Dürn	22.4.19		Inspected animals of 186th Bde. & the following units:– 437 (S.R.E.) 461 R.E. 5th 1st Gordons 524 T.R.A.S.C. 181st T.M. 184 T.M. also D/310 R.F.A. Visited ringworm animals at the Concentration Camp Dürn.	W.H.P.
"	23.4.19		Inspected all animals of Div. H.Q. Inspected for the purpose of ordering 29 veteran horses of Yeoman Airlines parade at Hull N.a.m. Visited of West Riding M.V.S. Inspected 3/10th 3/12th Bdes. Arty. at Gronau. Brought back 3 returnable cases from M.V.S. to transport to W.R. Guards Division to proceed to England following day to demobilisation. Visited A.D.V.S.	W.H.P.
"	24.4.19		Visited Horse Concentration Camp Dürn, & M.S.C. in Smithfields. Visited A.D.V.S. Proceeded to Sollet to attend sale for M.V.S. – trade very suitable class in the village.	W.H.P.
"	25.4.19		Staff-Sergeant Saxby clerk to D.A.D.V.S. demobilised proceeded to W.R. to-day. Pte Kennedy learn who has over Hutton for cases of M.V.S. yesterday has returned to-day. Visited A.D.V.S.	W.H.P.
"	26.4.19		Visited M.V.S. at Sollet. Inspected animals at Div. R.E. on loan to be transferred to M.V.S. Inspected animals at 3rd Bde. (H.Q. & sheets) Sgt. Blackwell R.A.V.C. – enlisted.	W.H.P.
"	27.4.19		Routine duties. Visited A.D.V.S.	W.H.P.
"	28.4.19		Headquarters Highland Division including D.A.D.V.S. Office moved to Kokozau. Visited ringworm animals at Concentration Camp Dürn. Visited ringworm animals at M.G.C. Dürn, two lorries transferred sick to M.V.S. Visited M.V.S. at Sollet.	W.H.P.
"	29.4.19		Routine duties.	W.H.P.
"	30.4.19		Inspected animals in Div. H.Q. at Brayton – visited ringworm animals at animal concentration Camp Dürn.	W.H.P.

W.H.Preston Capt. R.A.V.C.
* D.A.D.V.S.
Highland (visitor)

Original

Confidential

War Diary
of
D.A.Q.V.S.
Highland Division

From 1.5.19 To 31-5-19

Vol. XXIX

Army Form C. 2113.

WAR DIARY
INTELLIGENCE SUMMARY.
(Erase heading not required.)

Volume XXIX

Place	Date	Hour	Summary of Events and Information	Remarks and references to Appendices
Florina	1-5-19		Routine duties. Monthly returns completed.	
"	2-5-19		Visited M.V.S. Inspected animals of D.A.C. at Hall. Inspected animals of 526 Coy. R.A.S.C.	W.T.P.
"	3-5-19		Routine duties. Visited & inspected 350 animals at horse collecting Camp Dverin, prior to being sent by train to the base. Inspected Lines at 2nd Highland Bde. H.Q.	W.T.P.
"	4-5-19		Routine duties - unsported addition horse affected with mange at Fruzion.	W.T.P.
"	5-5-19		Visited & inspected animals at M.E.C. also Divn. R.E. Signals. Set a hand opthinia to veterinar of Dt. morton R.E. was unable to be opperated showing heart, at R.E. stables. Inspected all animals as D.M.E.	W.T.P.
"	6-5-19		Inspected animals at horse Collecting Camp Dverin. Visited M.K.S. at Sollar.	W.T.P.
"	7-5-19		Inspected animals of 527 Coy A.S.C. + 167 Bde. D/310 Bde R.F.A. Visited unsuspected animals at horse Collecting Camp Dverin.	W.T.P.
"	8-5-19		Handed over duties of D.A.D.V.S. Highland Division to Major Henry R.A.V.C.	W.T.P.
			W.H.Rotn Capt. R.A.V.C.	
"			Took over D.A.D.V.S. Highland Divn from Capt W.H. Rotn	
"	9-5-19		Visited ADVS IV Corps + 41 (WR) M.V.S. at SOLLER.	
"	10.5.19		Visited MVS. + 526 Coy RASC. Capt PRESTON to M.IV.VS. Compound. Instructed Capt. W.J. DARLING to proceed to 312 Fd. R.F.A. and take over the new change. Visited recent to Brunshije Capt. A.H. STROOD R.A.V.C at 310 Bde R.F.A	
"	12.5.19			

(A7091). Wt. W12593d/12373 75,000. 1/17. D. D. & L., Ltd. Forms/C2118/4.

WAR DIARY
INTELLIGENCE SUMMARY
(Erase heading not required.)

Army Form C. 2118.

Place	Date 1919	Hour	Summary of Events and Information	Remarks and references to Appendices
KREUTZAU	January 16.		Inspected 310 Bde RFA. Horses introduced but specialist and ancillary of Farriers. Being transferred to replace personnel. Stables are full of undisposed matters were completed. Arriving & suffering from lack of grooming & allowed to freeze. Inspected 2/Highland Field Transport (51 Canadian, 4 horses, 51 G.S. wagons)	Mwl
"	"	.4	Inspected 51 Half Bde — arrived yesterday. Capt. A.M. STROUD superintends demobilization.	
"	"	.19	With Cmpl HQ to see ADVS. Inspected 3rd Highland Bde Transport lost strength, 8Cpl ante. Visited ADS, 3-7H/18th weapons & motorists.	
"	"	.12	with ADVS.	
"	"	.14	Accompanied ADVS to 312 Bde RFA inspected horses, also 525 & 526 Cmp EASC	
"	"	.25	Inspected SMS horses then on my return to Cpt PRISTON (whom am from VS) In view of his proceeding tomorrow to IX Corps HQ to deputize for Mr Wrench to ADVS while he is on leave.	

Roland Langton
Lt./Col. V.O.

Army Form C. 2118.

WAR DIARY
or
INTELLIGENCE SUMMARY.

Original

(Erase heading not required.)

Instructions regarding War Diaries and Intelligence Summaries are contained in F.S. Regs., Part II. and the Staff Manual respectively. Title pages will be prepared in manuscript.

Place	Date	Hour	Summary of Events and Information	Remarks and references to Appendices
MEUZA V	25-5-19		Took over duties of D.A.D.V.S. Highland Division from Major Verney	WMP
"	26-5-19		Proceeded to Solau & took over command of 2/1 West Riding M.V.S. from Lt. Crowden R.A.V.C. who went on V.D. to 310th Bde. R.F.A. Inspected animals at H.Q. Signals R.E. Durin	WMP
"	27-5-19		Inspected animals at 460 Coy. R.E.s at BERG. Duty with M.V.S.	WMP
"	28-5-19		Inspected animals of 2/3 W.R. Field Ambulance Durin. 461 Coy. R.E.s.	WMP
"	29-5-19		Routine duties. Duty with M.V.S.	WMP
"	30-5-19		Visited inspected animals at various Collecting Camps Durin. Interviewed A.D.V.S. at TV Copa. Accompanied A.D.V.S. to inspect M.V.S.	WMP
"	31-5-19		Duty with M.V.S.	WMP

W.S. Renton Capt. R.A.V.C.
a/D.A.D.V.S.
Highland Division

Original

62 DIV

Confidential

War Diary
of
D.A.D.V.S
Highland Division

From 1-5-19   To 31-5-19

Vol. XXIX

WAR DIARY
or
INTELLIGENCE SUMMARY.

Army Form C. 2118.

Place	Date	Hour	Summary of Events and Information	Remarks and references to Appendices
			Vol. XXIX	
Fragano	1.5.19		Routine duties. Monthly returns completed	W.D.P.
"	2.5.19		Visited M.V.S. Inspected animals of DAC at Hell. Inspected animals	W.D.P.
"	3.5.19		Routine duties. Visited & inspected 300 animals at Horse Collecting Camp. Division horse is being sent by train to the base. Inspected Lorry at 52nd Highland Bde H.Q.	W.D.P.
"	4.5.19		Routine duties - inspected civilian horse affected with mange at Fragano	W.D.P.
"	5.5.19		Visited inspected animals at M.V.S. also Div R.E. Signals. Set a round of opinion to ascertain if Dr. master R.E. are suitable to be appointed Veterinary Sect at R.E. stables. Inspected all animals at D.M.V.	W.D.P.
"	6.5.19		Inspected animals at Horse Collecting Camp Division. Visited M.V.S.-Selles.	W.D.P.
"	7.5.19		Inspected animals of 527th Bty A.T.C. + 167th Bde. D/310 F.Bde R.F.A. Visited inspected animals at Horse Collecting Camp Division	W.D.P.
"	8.5.19		Handed over duties of D A D V S. Highland Division to Major Harvey R.A.V.C.	W.D.P.

W H Pinton
Capt R.A.V.C.

"	9.5.19		Took over HQ Highland Div't from Capt W H Pinton. Visited ADM IV Corps & M(W) MVS at SULEN.	
"	10.5.19		Visited MVS + 326 Coy RASC Instructed Capt W J Dorling to proceed to 3rd Fd. Ride RFA and take in veterinary matters. Received to Ammunition Capt A H STROUD RAVC at 310th RFA	

WAR DIARY
or
INTELLIGENCE SUMMARY.

Army Form C. 2118.

Place	Date	Hour	Summary of Events and Information	Remarks and references to Appendices
KREUZLAU	1918 May 16		[handwritten entries, largely illegible]	
	17			
	19			
	22			
	24			
	26			

Army Form C. 2118.

WAR DIARY or INTELLIGENCE SUMMARY.

(Erase heading not required)

Original

Place	Date	Hour	Summary of Events and Information	Remarks and references to Appendices
MEUZA U	25.5.19		Took over duties of D.A.D.V.S. Highland Division from Major Vinney	
"	26.5.19		Proceeded to Solliers + took over command of H.Q. 51st Railway M.V.S. from Lt. Crawford R.A.V.C. who came in F.O. in 31st Feb. R.T.A.	
"	27.5.19		Inspected animals at 466 Coy R.E. at BERG. Duts with M.V.S.	
"	28.5.19		Inspected animals of 75 W.R Field Ambulance Division. 461 Coy R.E.S.	
"	29.5.19		Routine duties. Duts with M.V.S.	
"	30.5.19		Visited unspected animals at Animal Collecting Comps Division Interviewed A.D.V.S. at Tel Stepo accompanied A.D.V.S. to inspect M.V.S.	
"	31.5.19		Duty with M.V.S.	

W H Fort Capt R.A.V.C.
A/D.A.D.V.S.
Highland Division

Original

Confidential
War Diary
of
D.A.D.V.S
Highland Division
from 1.6.19   To 30.6.19

Vol. XXVIII

Army Form C. 2118.

WAR DIARY
or
INTELLIGENCE SUMMARY.
(Erase heading not required.)

Instructions regarding War Diaries and Intelligence Summaries are contained in F.S. Regs., Part II. and the Staff Manual respectively. Title pages will be prepared in manuscript.

Place	Date	Hour	Summary of Events and Information	Remarks and references to Appendices
KREUZAU	1/6/19		Duty with M.V.S. also in Office D.A.D.V.S	WD
"	2/6/19		Duty with M.V.S. Inspected animals on Div. H.Q.	WD
"	3/6/19		Duty with M.V.S. Inspected animals of 6/5 Royal Highlanders; Div Coy. R.E. & at DUREN. Inspected animals of 457 Coy. R.E. & at Stockheim. Met O.i/c. Claims Office at SOLLER re mortgages damage done to pie to a C/R. and to spare parts.	WD
"	4/6/19		Duty with M.V.S. (Inspected) Sr. Lt. Gordons. D/310 Bde R.F.A. 62nd M.C.C. 2/2 M.R. Trawler also animals of 1/5th Gordons.	WD
"	5/6/19		Duty with M.V.S. also at D.A.D.V.S Office.	WD
"	6/6/19		Duty with M.V.S. also at D.A.D.V.S. Office.	WD
"	7/6/19		Duty with M.V.S. + D.A.D.V.S. Office.	WD
"	8/6/19		Duty with M.V.S. Inspected animals of 8/5 Black Watch + H.Q. 3rd Highland Bde.	WD
"	9/6/19		Duty with M.V.S. Inspected animals of 310th + 312th Bdes R.F.A. also 5/25" + 5/26" 6/pr. R.A.S.C. Had a matter of broad mortgages at Turflspore. I render officers of the appoint claims there.	WD
"	10/6/19		Duty with M.V.S. inspected animals of Divl Signals R.E. at DUREN. D in H.Q. Visited sick animal at UNT-MAUBACH of 6th Black Watch.	WD
"	11/6/19		Duty with M.V.S. Routine duties to the Base.	WD
"	12/6/19		Duty with M.V.S. Inspected animals of Sr. 2nd Gordons. D.A.C. required 24 2/5th Seaforths	WD
"	13/6/19		Duty with M.V.S. Routine duties in the Office	WD

Army Form C. 2118.

WAR DIARY
or
INTELLIGENCE SUMMARY.
(Erase heading not required.)

Instructions regarding War Diaries and Intelligence Summaries are contained in F. S. Regs., Part II. and the Staff Manual respectively. Title pages will be prepared in manuscript.

Place	Date	Hour	Summary of Events and Information	Remarks and references to Appendices
KREUZAU	14/6/19		Duty with M.V.S. Routine duties in the Office.	
"	15/6/19		Duty with M.V.S. Routine duties in the Office.	
"	16/6/19		Duty with M.V.S. Routine duties in the Office.	
"	17/6/19		Duty with M.V.S. Inspected animals at Div. H.Q. & 6th Black Watch.	
"	18/6/19		Duty with M.V.S. Inspected animals of 457th Coy R.E. & 226th Coy R.A.S.C.	
"	19/6/19		Duty with M.V.S. Routine duties in the Office.	
"	20/6/19		Duty with M.V.S. Routine duties in the Office.	
"	21/6/19		Duty with M.V.S. Routine duties in the Office.	
"	22/6/19		Duty with M.V.S. Routine duties in the Office.	
"	23/6/19		Duty with M.V.S. Inspected animals of Div. Art. H.Q.	
"			Handed over duties of D.A.D.V.S. to Major Roney, D.S.O., who returned from Teplitz, and proceeded to Corps.	
"	24/6/19		Routine duties.	
"	25/6/19		Routine duties. Visited & inspected 2/i/c W.R. M.V.S.	
"	26/6/19		Routine duties.	
"	27/6/19		Routine duties. Visited M.P. Corps. Animal Collecting Camp DUREN	
"	28/6/19		Routine duties. Visited 2/i/c W.R. M.V.S.	
"	29/6/19		Routine duties.	
"	30/6/19		Handed over duties of D.A.D.V.S. to Capt. W.H. Proud, P.M.C. Proceeded to U.K. on 14 days Leave.	

30-6-19

Original

Confidential

War Diary

of

D.A.D.V.S

Highland Division

From 1/6/19   To 30.6.19

Vol XXVIII

Army Form C. 2118.

WAR DIARY
or
INTELLIGENCE SUMMARY.
(Erase heading not required.)

Instructions regarding War Diaries and Intelligence Summaries are contained in F. S. Regs., Part II. and the Staff Manual respectively. Title pages will be prepared in manuscript.

OFFICER-IN-CHARGE RECORDS
1 JAN 1920
ROYAL ARMY VET. CORPS

Place	Date	Hour	Summary of Events and Information	Remarks and references to Appendices
RITZAU	1/6/19		Duty with M.V.S. also in office DADVS	
"	2/6/19		Duty with M.V.S. Inspected animals in Div. HQ.	
"	3/6/19		Duty with M.V.S. Inspected animals of 9.C. Royal Highlanders: Div. Cav. R.E. at DUREN. R.E.S. at Shooteven. M.T.-D.S. Annex open at SOLLER. A.S. Inspected animals of 4,5,7 Coy R.E.S. at Shooteven to investigate damage done by fire to a C.T. used as cook-house.	
"	4/6/19		Duty with M.V.S. Inspected 8/1, L. Gordons. D/300 Bde R.F.A. 62nd M.C.C. 2/2 W.R. T Ambce also animals of 1/5th Gordons.	
"	5/6/19		Duty with M.V.S. also at DADVS office	
"	6/6/19		Duty with M.V.S. also at DADVS office.	
"	7/6/19		Duty with M.V.S & DADVS office.	
"	8/6/19		Duty with M.V.S. Inspected animals of B & E Black Watch & M.G. 3rd Highland Bde.	
"	9/6/19		Duty with M.V.S. Inspected animals of 310th + 312th Bdes R.F.A. also 515th + 526th Coys R.A.S.C. Had a interview of brass conducted at Forstshove to consider efficiency of mean to be adopted during trial.	
"	10/6/19		Duty with M.V.S. inspected animals of Divnl. Signals R.E.I. at DUREN. D.w.H.Q. visited Sick animals at W.H.T.-M.T.-R.A.C.H. D. & E. Black Watch.	
"	11/6/19		Duty with M.V.S. Routine duties in the office	
"	12/6/19		Duty with M.V.S. Inspected animals of 51st Gordons. D.A.C. Highland Divl. 1/6 Seaforths.	
"	13/6/19		Duty with M.V.S. Routine duties in the office	

Army Form C. 2118.

WAR DIARY
or
INTELLIGENCE SUMMARY.
(Erase heading not required.)

Instructions regarding War Diaries and Intelligence Summaries are contained in F.S. Regs., Part II. and the Staff Manual respectively. Title pages will be prepared in manuscript.

OFFICER-IN-CHARGE RECORDS
1 JAN 1920
ROYAL ARMY VET[ERINARY]

Place	Date	Hour	Summary of Events and Information	Remarks and references to Appendices
AREQUA	14/6/19		Duty with M.V.S. Routine duties in the Office.	
"	16/6/19		Duty with M.V.S. Routine duties in the Office.	
"	16/6/19		Duty with M.V.S. Routine duties in the Office.	
"	17/6/19		Duty with M.V.S. Inspected animals at Det. H.Q. + 6" B'ade Wksh.	
"	18/6/19		Duty with M.V.S. Inspected animals of 437"/6y R.E. + 3.28"/6y RASC	
"	19/6/19		Duty with M.V.S. Routine duties in the Office.	
"	20/6/19		Duty with M.V.S. Routine duties in the Office.	
"	21/6/19		Duty with M.V.S. Routine duties in the Office.	
"	22/6/19		Duty with M.V.S. Routine duties in the Office.	
"	23/6/19		Duty with M.V.S. Inspected animals of Det. Amb + 9	
"	24/6/19		Handed over duties of DADVS to Major Morris D.S.O who relieved from Tripn. dutys wADVS 16 Corps	
"	25/6/19		Routine duties	
"	2-16/6/19		Routine duties. Visited + inspected 3/1 W.R.N.V.S.	
"	26/6/19		Routine duties.	
"	27/6/19		Routine duties. Visited M.V. Cols. anneal Pilferlery Trinfo DUREN	
"	28/6/19		Routine duties. Visited 1/1 W R.M.V.S.	
"	29/6/19		Routine duties.	
"	30/6/19		Handed over duties of DADVS to Capt. W.H. Pinch DADVS. Proceeded to UK on 14 days leave.	

(A7092) Wt. W12559/M1293 75,000. 1/17. D.D. & L., Ltd. Forms/C2118.74.

Confidential.

WAR DIARY

OF

D.A.D.V.S. HIGHLAND Division.

From 1st July 1919.

To 31st July 1919.

(Volume XXVII)

Army Form C. 2118.

WAR DIARY
INTELLIGENCE SUMMARY.
(Erase heading not required.)

Instructions regarding War Diaries and Intelligence Summaries are contained in F. S. Regs., Part II. and the Staff Manual respectively. Title pages will be prepared in manuscript.

(TADS H D) Vol. 28.) from 1/7/19 to 31/7/19 Summary of Events and Information

Place	Date 1919	Hour	Summary of Events and Information	Remarks and references to Appendices
KREUZAU	July 1		Route work	*illegible*
	" 2		"	*illegible*
	" 3		"	*illegible*
	" 4		Occupied APO II Cafés inspecting 312 Bde RFA.	*illegible*
	" 5		ADVS Rhine Army inspected 31 (W.R.) M.V.S. Route work.	*illegible*
	" 7		"	*illegible*
	" 8		"	*illegible*
	" 9		"	*illegible*
	" 10		"	*illegible*
	" 11		"	*illegible*
	" 12		"	*illegible*
	" 13		"	*illegible*
	" 14		Major Vernon DADVS returned from leave to U.K. Have Certificate Board examined men with TADVS as a member for reclaiming all animals T, E, & S.	*illegible*
	" 15			
	" 16			
	" 17		Occupied a Certificate Board all men.	*illegible*
	" 18			*illegible*

WAR DIARY
INTELLIGENCE SUMMARY.
(Erase heading not required.)

Army Form C. 2118.

Place	Date	Hour	Summary of Events and Information	Remarks and references to Appendices
KREUZAU	July 19		Intelligence Branch at work.	[appx]
	20			[appx]
	21		Lieut. N. MACLEOD R.A.F. departed on leave to U.K. for protracted period. Intelligence Branch dismantled & all records & maps turned in.	[appx]
	22			[appx]
	23			[appx]
	26		} Routine work.	
	31			

Cmdr...
1st US Highland Div

Confidential.

War Diary
of
D.A.D.W.S. Highland Division

From 1.8.19.   To 31.8.19.

(Volume XXXII.)

Army Form C. 2118.

WAR DIARY
or
INTELLIGENCE SUMMARY.
(Erase heading not required.)

Instructions regarding War Diaries and Intelligence Summaries are contained in F. S. Regs., Part II. and the Staff Manual respectively. Title pages will be prepared in manuscript.

Place	Date	Hour	Summary of Events and Information	Remarks and references to Appendices
	1919		(BEF'S Highland Div Vol.29.)	
KREUZAU	Aug 1		Wired MVS	Cert
"	" 2		Routine work.	
"	" 3		" "	
"	" 4		Inspected 312 Bde RFA	
"	" 5		Routine work	
"	" 6		MVS + Hellenic going home to go on to England	
"	" 7		Routine work	
"	" 8		At General Collecting Camp and saw various Hellenic + hrs of leaving going to Cologne	
"	" 9		Left DUREN 6.30 P.M. via BHQ	
"	" 10		Arrived CALAIS 8 am. Rested 12 P.M. arrived Folkestone 2 P.M.	
"	" 11		returned to Clipstone Camp 8 P.M. arrived in ANTWERP	
CLIPSTONE	" 12			
"	" 28		demobilized at RAVC Kennels No 3 which before July 1916	
"	" 31		was attached to BEF's Highland Div and sent across.	

Lieut Colonel
BEF's H.D.

(A7091) Wt. W12859/M1293 75,000 1/17. D. D. & L., Ltd. Forms/C.2118/14.